MANCHESTER
UNIVERSITY PRESS

ISSUES IN GERMAN POLITICS

Edited by

Professor Charlie Jeffery, Institute for German Studies
Dr Charlie Lees, University of Sussex

Issues in German Politics is a major new series on contemporary Germany. Focusing on the post-unity era, it presents concise, scholarly analyses of the forces driving change in domestic politics and foreign policy. Key themes will be the continuing legacies of German unification and controversies surrounding Germany's role and power in Europe. The series includes contributions from political science, international relations and political economy.

Already published:

Bulmer, Jeffery and Paterson: *Germany's European diplomacy: Shaping the regional milieu*

Hyde-Price: *Germany and European order: Enlarging NATO and the EU*

Lees: *The Red–Green coalition in Germany: Politics, personalities and power*

Forthcoming titles include:

Jeffery: *The German Länder and the European Union*

Harnisch and Maull: *Germany as a civilian power*

Rittberger: *German Foreign Policy since unification*

The future of the German economy

An end to the miracle?

Edited by Rebecca Harding
and William E. Paterson

Manchester University Press
Manchester and New York
Distributed exclusively in the USA by St. Martin's Press

Published by Manchester University Press
Oxford Road, Manchester M13 9NR, UK
and Room 400, 175 Fifth Avenue, New York, NY 10010, USA
http/www.manchesteruniversitypress.co.uk

Distributed exclusively in the USA by
St. Martin's Press, Inc., 175 Fifth Avenue, New York,
NY 10010,USA

Distributed exclusively in Canada by
UBC Press, University of British Columbia, 2029 West Mall,
Vancouver, BC, Canada V6T 1Z2

British Library Cataloguing-in-Publication Data
A catalogue record for this book is available from the British Library

Library of Congress Cataloging-in-Publication Data applied for

ISBN 0 7190 5995 X *hardback*
0 7190 6010 9 *paperback*

First published 2000

07 06 05 04 03 02 01 00 10 9 8 7 6 5 4 3 2 1

Typeset in Minion
by Northern Phototypesetting Co. Ltd, Bolton
Printed in Great Britain
by Bell & Bain Ltd, Glasgow

Contents

Tables

Figures

Preface

At a dinner party, twenty years ago two professors, one German and one British, were making conversation. 'How is it,' asked the English professor, 'that Germany has performed so well economically in comparison to Britain?' The German professor thought carefully for a moment and then said, 'Oh, the answer is quite simple. In Germany, we do it better.'

In the intervening period, unemployment has risen to unprecedented levels. The difficulties of unification with the former German Democratic Republic were under-estimated and still plague macroeconomic indicators. And there are signs that consensus, so central to the German political culture and economic performance, is beginning to erode. Germany's own confidence about its ability to compete has waned. Politicians have sought inspiration from Anglo-US structures rather than German. And commentators from outside of Germany with, perhaps, more than a touch of *Schadenfreude* have pointed to the decline of the German model as a means of economic organisation.

Against this background, we, as two British commentators, have decided to edit a book which paints a relatively optimistic picture of Germany's future. Why? How can we remain positive when, apparently, hard evidence is against us? Do we not see the true extent to which the German model is crumbling under the dual pressures of globalisation and unification. We do, of course, see the German model adapting to globalisation, but argue that adaptation is inherent to the German model.

Our reasons for being positive stem from the very 'Britishness' that might, to an 'insider', make our commentary seem too rosy. We come from a political culture where individualism and markets have been dominant for the last twenty years. The frontiers of the State have been 'rolled back'. At the beginning of the twenty-first century British government policy towards the economy still rests on an assumption that, if prices and costs are kept low, then firms (and hence the economy) will be competitive. Inward investment is to be encouraged in order to teach our companies the rules of the global era.

The result is under-investment in innovation and education, an industrial relations structure which would have been unrecognisable twenty years ago and capital markets and corporate strategies which are so dictated to by the concept of shareholder value that the concept of 'long-termism' can sometimes be deemed a synonym for uncompetitiveness. Small and large companies in traditional manufacturing regions struggle to survive because of the high value of Sterling and our export performance is, of course, usually in manufacturing. Structures designed to help innovation and business start-ups, particularly venture capital, are so dominated by the need to pay good returns, that they fail to provide appropriate finance to the companies that really need it.

Yet alongside this there is a real and rather insular arrogance about British economic performance remains. Yes, in terms of macroeconomic indicators we are doing well. Inflation is low as is unemployment and economic growth has been high since the late 1990s. British labour markets are flexible (in other words trade unions have little power left and wages are comparatively low). But Britons ignore more worrying trends in the micro economy at their peril. It is here, in the long run, where competitiveness is created, where innovation is generated, where the infrastructure supports businesses small and large and, ultimately, where politicians are really judged.

We are firmly of the view that British politicians need to look again at the *enabling* role of the state in stimulating competitiveness and growth. Germany has learnt many lessons about the strengths and weaknesses of corporatism. German politicians and businesses alike have learned how to add shareholder value to their list of *stakeholders* and, hence, to incorporate some of the criteria of competitiveness in a global era into the supposedly rigid structures of the consensual model.

We make no apology for being positive. The style of this book is, generally, lively and up-beat. The material is balanced. We do not deny that there are problems, and the contribution by Lothar Funk is generally pessimistic. Indeed, we urge policy-makers to deal with structural unemployment with some urgency. But this is, we hope, a book which will rebalance comment on the German economy. We must guard against complacency in the UK and there are, undoubtedly, still powerful policy lessons to be learnt as this large economy adapts successfully to change.

Finally, it remains only to thank the people who have been involved with this book. All of the contributors have produced high quality material to tight deadlines and within busy schedules. We are indebted to Ray Cunningham of the Anglo–German Foundation and to David Marsh of Hawkpoint Partners and the German–British Forum for providing us with places to meet in London. Gundula Campden passed frantic messages, e-mails and faxes between us with astonishing patience. And finally the biggest thanks goes to our partners and families who provided tea, sympathy and space during the seemingly endless task of putting the manuscript together – we would not have done this without you. Any errors of judgement remain, of course, our own.

Rebecca Harding, William E. Paterson

Contributors

Louise Amoore Louise Amoore gained her Ph.D from the Department of Politics, University of Newcastle in 1998. She is now a lecturer in International Political Economy at the University of Northumbria, Newcastle-upon-Tyne. Her work has been published in *Global Society, New Political Economy* and the *Review of International Political Economy.* She is currently researching the relationship between social experiences of production and work and processes of globalisation.

Lothar Funk Lothar Funk obtained his Ph.D in Economics in 1996 from the University of Trier where he is now a post-doctoral fellow. He has been seconded to the Institute of German Studies at the University of Birmingham where he is currently the German Academic Exchange Service (DAAD) Senior Fellow in Economics. His most recent publications include two books on the 'Third Way' (1999, 2000).

Rebecca Harding Rebecca Harding is a Senior Lecturer at the Science and Technology Policy Research Unit (SPRU), University of Sussex and a research associate of the Institute for Public Policy Research (IPPR) in London. She has research, consultancy and policy experience in innovation management, innovation systems, industrial relations and venture capital in Germany and Britain. She is a policy advisor to the Regional Innovation Strategy of Altmark–Harz–Magdeburg, advises the Irish Cross Border Policy Committee on venture capital development and has worked in an advisory capacity to the Fraunhofer Society.

Her books include *Technology and Human Resource Strategies in their National Context* (1995), *One Semester Economics* (1998), *Venture Capital and Regional Development* (1999) and *Knowledge Links: Innovation in University/business Partnerships* (with Steve Lissenburgh) (2000). She has also published extensively in journals including the *British Journal of*

Management, Technovation, German Politics and the *National Institute Economic Review*, largely from research comparing and contrasting German and British technology and R&D strategies and corporate structures.

David Marsh David Marsh has worked at Reuters Newsagency and the *Financial Times* as a European correspondent in London, Paris and Germany. In 1995 he became Director of European Strategy at Robert Fleming and in December 1998 moved to work in the corporate finance department. He is presently Vice Chairman of Hawkpoint Partners, a corporate finance house based in London.

David Marsh is an Honorary Professor of the University of Birmingham, and a Member of the Board of Trustees, Centre for European Reform, the Board of Trustees, Dresden Trust and the Königswinter Conference Steering Committee. He is also Deputy Chairman of the German–British Forum and winner of the Anglo–German Foundation annual journalism award in 1988 and the David Holden correspondence prize in 1989.

He has written three books: *The Germans: Rich, Bothered and Divided* (1989), *The Bundesbank: The Bank that Rules Europe* (1992) and *Germany and Europe: The Crisis of Unity* (1994).

William E. Paterson William Paterson began his academic career as a Lecturer in Politics and International Relations at the University of Aberdeen and later moved to the University of Warwick as a Volkswagen Lecturer where, after a number of years, he was promoted to a Professorship in Politics. In 1990 he returned home to Scotland and to the University of Edinburgh where he was appointed Salvesen Professor of European Institutions and Director of the University's Europa Institute.

In 1994 he was enticed south to Birmingham to head the Institute for German Studies where he has been especially committed to the idea of the Institute being a dedicated centre of research excellence, a genuine postgraduate community and a key contributor to the on-going British–German policy debate.

He has written or edited over twenty books and a large number of academic papers on European and German issues. In addition to his other activities and responsibilities he is a co-editor of *German Politics*; he is a member of the British Steering Committee of the Königswinter Conferences, a member of the Advisory Council (Beirat) of the Grossbrittanien Zentrum of the Humboldt Universität, Berlin, and is Deputy Chairman of the UK's German–British Forum.

In recognition of his 'outstanding contribution to British–German relations', Professor Paterson was awarded the German Order of Merit in March 1999. In June 1999 he received an OBE in the Queen's Birthday Honours List.

Arndt Sorge Arndt Sorge is Professor of Organisation Structuring at the University of Groningen, The Netherlands. He has worked on the organisation and management of industrial enterprises, vocational education and training, personnel policy and industrial relations. This has included a number of empirical international comparisons, and a focus on the development and utilisation of new technology. Since 1972, he has held academic positions in Germany, England, France and the Netherlands. He was recently editor-in-chief of *Organization Studies* (1996-99), and of the Organization section and spin-offs of the *International Encyclopedia of Business and Management* (Routledge and subsequently Thomson Publishing).

David Soskice David Soskice is Director of the Research Area, 'Employment and Economic Change' at the Wissenschaftszentrum für Sozialforschung, Berlin (WZB). He is also Emeritus Fellow of Economics, University College, Oxford, Adjunct Research Professor, Research School of the Social Sciences, Australian National University and Research Associate, with responsibility for coordination of long-term policy on post-16 education and training, Prime Minister's Policy Unit, 10, Downing Street.

He has previously held many positions including posts at Cornell University, University of California at Berkeley, Harvard, Stanford and Duke University. He has also acted as an advisor to HM Treasury, to the OECD and various European governments. He has published four books and over thirty articles and papers in the area of employment and economic change.

Graham Timmins Graham Timmins is Senior Lecturer in Politics at the University of Stirling. He has published widely on European and German Politics. Recent publications include, *German Unification and Organised Labour: Social Partnership Under Pressure* (forthcoming), *The EU and NATO enlargement Processes in Comparative Perspective* (co-authored with Martin Smith) (2000).

1
Germany in a global era

Rebecca Harding and William E. Paterson

Nay but tell me in our traces
Are we standing or advancing?
All is whirling, swimming, dancing,
Fell and forest, full of faces, mock at us.
(Goethe, *Faust*, Part I)

Introduction: the performance paradox

Germany woke up stunned on the morning after the general election in September 1998. 'I can't believe what we have done,' a friend said, 'we have voted for change. We have voted for something different.' This palpable shock was equalled only by the sentiments on the morning after the Berlin Wall came down, when, 'it was plain [that] everyone understood that something undreamt of and enormous was happening' (Porter 1999).

In the intervening period since the fall of the Wall and the 1998 general election, Germany may appear to be in crisis. Wirtschaftwoche's *Schröder Uhr* ticks away relentlessly measuring weekly employment changes since Gerhard Schröder came to power. It has, until recently, shown no noticeable improvement in the numbers unemployed and still indicates a downward trend in the total size of the work force. For a government prepared to be judged on the basis of its record on unemployment this makes alarming reading. Taxes (particularly corporation tax) are argued to be uncompetitive and labour markets to be inflexible. And, if this were not enough, the confused electorate views the government's progress on welfare reform as limited, sees the 'Red–Green coalition' as being in shreds and blames the SPD's electoral disasters since September 1998 on Schröder's personal lack of credibility (*Der Spiegel*, 44/1999, pp. 22–30).

Is Germany really in crisis? Are we seeing the end of the post-war German economic miracle that has created a solid economic infrastructure, low unemployment until reunification with eastern Germany, low inflation and strong export performance? Certainly the macroeconomic indicators appear to point in that direction and, were that the case, the German electorate's dismay would be understandable.

A closer examination of the facts, leads to rather different conclusions. Yes, there are macroeconomic problems. Indeed, it would be disingenuous to suggest that these are unimportant, not least because they are the issues that are paramount in people's minds when they judge their political leaders. Unemployment remains stubbornly high at 9.8 per cent of total employment. Yet alongside this, inflation is low at 1.1 per cent, annual growth in GDP is predicted to be 2.4 per cent during the year 2000, public sector finances have substantially improved over the five years since 1995 and the balance of payments is in surplus. The innovation infrastructure in Germany is remarkably strong, and there is evidence that strong export performance over the last two years is beginning to filter through into higher aggregate demand and, as a result, unemployment is predicted to fall during the year 2000 (DIW, 2000). German companies have increasingly over the last ten years shifted their base from domestic to global operations and continue to be highly competitive in world markets, evidenced by the strong export performance which in itself is helped by the weak value of the euro. Even in newer areas, like Information and Communication Technology (ICT) and biotechnology, and new service sectors, like venture capital, Germany has become something of a policy ideal for injecting dynamism and change (Harding 1999b; Lissenburgh and Harding 2000; Casper 1998; Adelberger 2000). So much is this the case that, at a recent meeting on UK policy towards venture capital, a representative of the largest British venture capital company, 3i, suggested that Germany was something of a role model in this sector.

This is the essence of the Performance Paradox (Harding 1999a). Evidence that the German economy is strong is equally as compelling as the evidence that it is not strong. Authors point on the one hand to institutional inflexibility and, on the other, to inherent dynamism in the system. For example, Mannesmann has been taken over by Vodafone–Airtouch, but equally, Germany has the highest numbers of people wanting to set up their own businesses in Europe (*FT* 17 Feb. 2000). Similarly, there is evidence that Germany's has benefited from the low value of the euro to a significant degree, yet this positive fact hides the need for, and indeed displaces, structural reform. So why, if microeconomic indicators are so strong, and even macroeconomic indicators are improving, is there such a strong feeling of pessimism about the future of the German 'model' both within Germany and outside it?

This paradox can be resolved in two ways – one social, the other analytical. First, the social aspect of the problem. Unemployment is a central issue. Western Germans over the age of 25 have grown up with the expectation that their education, carefully combining vocational and academic qualifications, would lead them inevitably to secure jobs and a high standard of living. A *Kur*, provided through their health insurance, ensured their mental as well as physical well-being. Similarly, eastern Germans of a comparable age were guaranteed jobs within the Communist system, if not with the same standard of living then with equal security.

Suddenly their world is imperilled. The global, knowledge-based economy modelled on an Anglo-Saxon order popularly appears to have superseded *Modell Deutschland* and politicians seem powerless to do anything about it. Employment can no longer be taken for granted. The health and social security system are in crisis. Just six months after the election Germany found itself involved in military combat in mainland Europe for the first time since the Second World War and fighting at the behest of a Red–Green alliance. It was not surprising, then, that this led to dissatisfaction and confusion.

But dissatisfaction, confusion and even pessimism are not strangers in German history. One need only look at the Romantic movement in art, music and literature to demonstrate this! As Marsh argues later in this book, West Germans have a weak record of radical change after their successful transition from dictatorship to democracy in the first post-war years and surprise themselves when they do something quickly or differently. Economic institutions tend to reflect this and the incrementalism of the German 'model' is well-documented (Soskice 1994; Carlin and Soskice 1997; Casper *et al.* 1999; Vitols, 1997). There has been real real doubt about the ability of Germany to adapt swiftly enough to a global order which is based on risk and rapid innovations (*Wirtschaftswoche*, 45.4 Nov. 1999 p. 30).

Yet arguably it is this self-doubt that drives the actors within the social, political and economic structures to adapt to changes successfully, and, if not quickly then incrementally, building on the structures that already exist. Eight years ago, senior managers at Bosch expressed deep concern at their relative lack of innovations (they were at the time number one in Europe) and at the forthcoming completion of the European single market, 'We're just not competitive enough to deal with it.' Lucas, on the other hand were confident, 'Oh, we innovate – people copy us. And 1992 – well, we've operated on a pan-European basis for years' (Harding 1995). Bosch is still number one in Europe. Lucas has been taken over by an American company.

This then leads to the second, analytical, aspect of the confusion when studying Germany. Analysts who examine macroeconomic data and predict some form of economic Armageddon, study quite different things to those who paint a more positive picture. 'Crisis' writers examine macroeconomic data as a product of dysfunction in particular parts of the model, particularly in policy, and argue that it is these faults which have caused the run of bad economic and social data. The difficulty with this approach lies in three basic assumptions.

- First, *Modell Deutschland* is seen as a post-war and largely West German phenomenon.
- Second, the 'social-market' aspects of the model can be adequately represented by an analysis of social policy trends and capital–labour relationships (represented through the industrial relations system).
- Finally, there is a causal link between positive macroeconomic data and effective operation of a system.

In contrast, 'institutional' writers examine the institutions and networks within the model at a micro level. They examine the functions, say, of the financial system or the innovation system or the system of corporate governance and discuss the inter-relatedness of actors in the German social market economy generally and the innovation system in particular (see, for example, Soskice 1994, 1996; Harding 1995; Freeman 1995). The focus is on the strengths of the German system, for example in creating and sustaining a capacity of incremental rather than radical innovation or in the consistent creation of a skilled labour force. The conclusion is that the inter-relationships within the model create a secure structure, albeit adaptive rather than dynamic. Indeed the incrementally adaptive capacity of the German social market economy is seen as its major strength, hence any change should be evolutionary in nature.

Both views regard change as inevitable and, to a greater or lesser extent, necessary. What is important, however, is not the changes that are taking place *in themselves*, but rather *how* those changes relate to the system itself and its sustainability. If there is indeed a *Market Economy* (as opposed to a social-market economy) developing, it implies that the 'core' of *Modell Deutschland* is diminishing, both in size and importance. Indeed, this change is necessary in order to compete in the Anglo-Saxon global market economy. However, if the changes are not external to the system but closely integrated into it, then the networks and inter-connectivities that are the base of the German model are still strong. The logical conclusion to this, latter argument is that the German capacity to generate growth based on long-termism, hi-tech product and process applications and incremental innovation remains formidable.

What we are examining in this book, then, are the effects of *exogenous* shocks on the 'German model'. The reunification of Germany is one such shock and 'globalisation' represents another. These have been the subject of huge attention and neurosis, both within and outside Germany. But our key purpose here is not to examine those shocks themselves but rather to assess their impact on the structures, systems and inter-connectivities associated with the German economic 'system'. The book as a whole is an attempt to resolve the performance paradox outlined above.

In order to begin to resolve the paradox, this chapter itself poses a number of questions. First, it asks, what are the key elements of the model, if indeed there is a model that accurately describes the structures of the German economy. It looks at individual structures commonly associated with Germany and highlights recent research which demonstrates the importance of these structures in the global strategies of large corporations. It goes on to argue, however, that although there clearly are important institutional structures, this does not imply that there is no change nor, indeed that they are uncompetitive as is commonly assumed.

Second, it asks the question, is there a 'global paradigm'? There is much discussion in the literature across a number of disciplines about the nature of globalisation and the impact that this has on the individual nation state. We argue that there are critical features of the current era in economic activity. In particular, it maintains, the key issue for the German economy is the requirement in the global era for speed to market, flexibility and entrepreneurial/risk-based behaviour as a means of enabling rapid and radical innovations.

Third, it goes on to ask, what is the role of the state in this global era? It suggests that the role of the state is in *enabling* risks to be taken – by cooperating at a supra-national level with other nation-states, by learning from policies elsewhere and, critically, by creating appropriate policy mechanisms and tools at a regional level. This enabling role is effected by national governments and involves both a pro-active attitude to risk *and* a clear balance between public and private sector involvement.

Finally, then, the critical question is asked, is Rhineland capitalism an alternative to the Anglo-Saxon global paradigm? It argues that the institutional structures of 'Rhineland capitalism' have major flaws in macro level coordination, particularly in reducing unemployment. But, this does not mean either that the model is static or that it is uncompetitive. As the case study of biotechnology and venture capital shows, the adaptive capacity of the structure is substantial.

What is essential in the global era is to view the definition of the state and its role in policy formulation as changing therefore. The role for industrial and micro-level policy is central in generating an innovative and dynamic base where previously macroeconomic issues dominated. While there may be good reasons to doubt the capacity of Germany's macro-institutions to change and, hence to generate full employment in the short term, there is little doubt that the strengths of the economy and of policy are evident at a micro level.

Is there a 'model' of Rhineland capitalism?

> They [Germany and America] showed no enthusiasm for the increasingly organised pattern of economic behaviour, replacing the older methods of arriving at decisions through the autonomous, if haphazard, movement of the market ...
>
> When Germans began to reconstruct their economy, they built upon the familiar structural foundation and plan, much of it invisible to the naked eye, as if guided by an archaeologist who could pick his way blind-fold through his favourite ruin. (Shonfeld 1969: 239, 236)

These two quotes strike at the heart of the features of the '*Modell Deutschland*' under discussion here. The organised, developed and quasi-coordinated structures of economic management at a macro and meso level combined with a historically based internationalism, integration and partnership between private and public sector institutions to produce the economic successes of the 1970s and early 1980s. Since the early 1980s however, as Funk points out in chapter 2, economic indicators have appeared less miraculous. Commentators from within Germany and from outside have raised serious questions about the sustainability of the 'model'.

So, is there a 'model'? Institutional writers would argue that there are clear and definable structures that characterise the German economy and that these can have a measurable effect on indigenous companies. Seminal work by the National Institute for Economic and Social Research demonstrates that sophisticated education and training, for example, leads to markedly higher productivity (Prais 1981; Daly *et al.* 1985; Mason *et al.* 1994; Mason and Wagner 1994, 1999). The structures under which the contents of education and training programmes are developed ensures that there is a reliable source of skills from which companies can recruit. Similarly, while producing undeniable rigidities, the stability of the relationship between trade unions, finance and management is designed to allow for long-term anticipation of and responses to changes in competitive conditions.

Indeed, attempts have been made recently to measure the impact of 'systemness' on the decision-making processes of large German companies (Mayer and Whittington 1999). Through a detailed study of the diversification strategies of the top 100 firms (by sales) in France, Germany and Britain, they argue that national differences are still important determining patterns of ownership, control and management development. Indeed, although large firms, arguably through their globalisation strategies, are becoming more similar 'in terms of diversification and specialisation … [they] are able to reconcile national institutions with international practices in a way that allows for both change and continuity' (Mayer and Whittington 1999: 933). Thus, for example, between 1983 and 1993:

- German companies have a heavy concentration of shareholdings in personal (rather than fund) investments and this has not changed significantly.
- Personal ownership of firms remains a significant feature of the industrial landscape.
- There is a strong dominance of technical qualifications as a means of internal promotion within firms.
- Between 1950 and 1993 the strategy of related diversification has dominated the decision-making of large German companies. However, over the same period, unrelated diversification has become increasingly important,

Research from various disciplines over a sustained period of time has clearly identified institutional features of the German economy which impact in a measurable way on the strategies and structures of indigenous companies. Casper *et al.* reinforce this in their work looking at developing biotechnology structures in Germany and the extent to which they are supported by national institutional structures. Like the Mayer and Whittington paper, they identify clear structures which underpin the emergence of that sector – for example, strong technology transfer links between industry and the science base in universities, high level skills and an emphasis on the development of process technologies. But, they argue, there are also signs that these structures are changing in favour of the development of innovation markets in Germany (Casper *et al.* 1999: 23; see also Adelberger 2000).

The inter-related nature of German institutions has given rise to the fascination with the German model throughout its industrial history. Its capacity to produce change while retaining its institutional structures is evident throughout. Thus, as Harding and Sorge argue in their chapter, there was evidence of 'modern' financial structures as early as as the mid-nineteenth century when the 'simultane Gründung' law allowed banks to take an equity stake in entrepreneur-based businesses and sell this stake when the firm was established. In twenty-first century terms, this is the essence of venture capital!

Perhaps the difficulty faced by commentators seeking to explain Germany's current competitive position, or to predict its future, lies in the fact that their focus is too narrow. As has already been pointed out, it is misleading simply to study macroeconomic indicators over a limited time period. It is similarly misleading to take too narrow a definition of the German 'model'. All too often the focus is on one aspect of that model – in particular, industrial relations and codetermination. The widest possible definition should be used to allow for the rich adaptive capacity of the *system* to be understood. Change is endemic and the critical question is not whether national systems adapt, but *how* (Duysters and Hagedoorn 1996).

So, for a book which is concerned with the *future* of the German economy, it is necessary both to look at its performance through past changes in paradigm *and* to look at its response now to any shifts in paradigm. It is misleading to look at any one point in time, therefore, and conclude that an economy will never recover, or, worse, that its 'model' no longer works. While this makes good copy for journalists, it is inadequate to understanding the real and complex processes at work within a particular nation state. An economy's future performance rests on its capacity to respond appropriately to the challenges posed by the exogenous changes over which it has little or no control.

Is there a global paradigm?

So is there a paradigm shift? That the world has become 'more global' is one of the clichés of the management literature. What is important about this phase, however, is the impact that it has on national structures which previous eras in the internationalisation of economic activity have not had. As Dunning argues, this in an era which,

> recognises no geographical boundaries [and which] ranges from changes in the way in which individual firms are organising their production and transactions, and the growing attention now being given to cross-border alliances and spatial networks, to the globalisation of economic activity and its impact on the role and policies of national governments and those of supranational institutions. (Dunning 1995)

Globalisation is, then, profoundly different to previous periods in international economic activity and has unique characteristics whose implications are analysed by Amoore in chapter 4 of this book. It would be neither appropriate nor necessary to enter into a detailed analysis here. Our concern is to highlight the key features which present particularly strong imperatives for adaptation generally and, hence, to map the potential adaptive capacity of Germany in particular. Broadly, these can be summarised as follows:

- *International networks and strategic alliances dominate.* Markets can no longer be relied upon to allocate resources efficiently and, instead, business and political organisations and institutions become interdependent.
- *Technology is central to the global era in that it both facilitates and drives the decision by companies to internationalise.* Very simply, it is technological change (and in particular information and communication technologies: ICT) that have made strategic communication on a global basis possible. But, equally, ICT is central to the latest swathe of global information technology (IT) and telecommunications companies that exploit internet and finance opportunities and 'grow global' apparently overnight.
- *Specialisation is central to developing and maintaining competitive and comparative advantage.* The internationalisation strategies of large companies generally and in particular the internationalisation of their research and development (R&D) rests on the desire to exploit technological strengths of their domestic base and to learn from expertise elsewhere (Cantwell and Harding 1998).
- *Speed of adaptation to new technologies and market conditions is critical* (Reich 1995). This means a proactive attitude to risk *and*, at a policy level, a high degree of partnership between the public and private sectors.

One more significant point warrants further exploration here. These features have commonly been associated with an 'Anglo-Saxon' (or at least American) paradigm that dominates the internationalisation of economic activity. A common assumption is that national boundaries are becoming less important in the corporate quest to reduce costs, increase quality and meet locally based customer requirements, as represented in the four key features listed above. *Adoption* of this paradigm is argued to be imperative for nation states seeking to retain competitive – there is 'One Best Way' of internationalising and competing in a global era.

However, this perspective is, arguably, a product of the 'comparative static' methodologies which were criticised above in that it ignores the process of historical and systemic *adaptation* over time (Lazonick 1991). By taking a multi-disciplinary approach comprising of economic, political, historical and institutional analysis it is possible to illustrate just how important this *adaptive* capacity is as a means for understanding how and why systems change. Further, understanding the nature and dynamic of this adaptive capacity is key for policy-makers wishing to formulate appropriate policies for future competitiveness.

What is the role of the state?

The role of policy in formulating the future of the German economy cannot – indeed should not – be understated given the integrated nature of the system generally and of the public and private sector in particular. Under a 'global' paradigm, then, what is the role of the state? There are, arguably, two levels upon which this role is enacted – a supra-national and national level.

At a supra-national level, the role of the state centres around coordination with other governments and ensuring that some form of 'policy learning' takes place. This does not mean ceding power to supra-national structures, although it may mean greater prominence for certain international elites (financiers in particular) (Dyson 2000). At a European policy level there is no evidence of 'fiscal federalism', no independent discretionary taxation, no centralised collective bargaining structures and no harmonised employment policy, for example. What it does mean, however, is a reinforced collaborative role for the state, both in terms of working with other international partners and in terms of learning from policies elsewhere (Dyson 2000).

This highlights the second area in which the state operates. At a national level, the role for the state in transferring effective policies to generate regional competitive advantage is key. Centrally, this concerns adapting best practice from elsewhere in the interests of stimulating growth, employment and innovation at a regional level. These are the features of strong industrial and regional policy. And, since these are both effected at the micro level of an economy, it is also the means of introducing dynamism and radical change – one of the critical features of competitiveness under the global paradigm.

In some senses this is a *redefinition* of the role of the state generally. Government policy under this structure has to be directed towards *enabling* effective market operations rather than intervening in markets. Policy makers have a role in identifying priorities and in creating infrastructures to facilitating their achievement. The strength of the state lies in its institutional structures that support these enabling policies.

Is Rhineland capitalism an alternative to the Anglo-Saxon paradigm?

Germany has, in the post-war period, operated on a European level as a coordinator. As Bulmer *et al.* argue:

> Germany is manifestly not a realist state pursuing its interests on specific issues on a case-by-case basis and acting accordingly as the realist paradigm would demand. Rather, Germany has pursued, in a more strategic sense, broad-based and diffuse milieu goals, directed at shaping wider conditions of inter-state interaction and, above all, cooperation beyond national boundaries. (Bulmer *et al.* 2000)

It is familiar with the dominance of a monetary elite and an independent central bank. This combined with its cooperative and coordinating approach should mean that its role at a supra-national level is embedded.

We propose, however, that the real strengths of *Modell Deutschland* or Rhineland capitalism are, and have always been, in the capacity at a policy level to identify strategic priorities. The achievement of those priorities is facilitated at a micro-industrial level through the provision both of enabling mechanisms and through the continued institutional strengths inherent to the system. Evidence from the biotechnology and venture capital sectors in Germany suggests that the State was, indeed, performing this task effectively during the 1990s in some key sectors (Adelberger 2000).

The scope of this book

The thrust of this book, then, is to examine the adaptive structures within the German economy and, hence, to derive some conclusions for policy in the final chapter. It aims to provide a picture of current issues and problems and to lend depth to this by detailed institutional and historical analysis. The individual chapters are ordered in a way that allows both a critical appraisal of current policy and a thorough historical examination of structural adaptation.

Chapter 2 is both an analytical and detailed coverage of the issues facing the German economy at the beginning of the twenty-first century. This chapter is the policy backdrop against which the durability of the German model is measured later in the text. Funk takes a pessimistic view of the policies of the Schröder administration to deal with unemployment and social reform – both key manifesto commitments. Since the election, he notes, the successes of the Red–Green coalition (measured in terms of opinion poll ratings) have been in reversing the Christian Democratic Union–Christian Social Union (CDU–CSU)'s unpopular social reforms but in terms of other, more forward-looking, policies, there has been very little progress. He argues that the persistently high unemployment stems, not from deficiencies in aggregate demand (although these have clearly played a part), but rather from rigidities and failings in the institutional structures of the social system. This leads to the inevitable conclusion that, without some form of social reform, substantial reductions in unemployment will be impossible. The weaknesses against the Anglo-Saxon model still persist in this area.

Timmins (chapter 3) develops the institutional perspective further in his analysis of the 'Alliance for Jobs' policy to reduce unemployment. He compares the 'Alliance for Jobs' with the 'Concerted Action' structures of the 1970s and sees evidence that the Alliance for Jobs faces similar constraints. There are two core strands to his discussion. First, like Funk, he maintains that current unemployment cannot be seen simply as a post-unification problem. Rather, inefficiencies in the institutional structures, here taken to be the industrial relations system, create endemic inflexibilities within the German labour market. Second, he argues that it is the fact that the 'Alliance for Jobs' reflects the traditional power structures within the industrial relations system that prevent the ability of it to create the dynamic changes that are necessary if unemployment is to be reduced.

The tone of these two chapters is in marked contrast to chapter 4, by

Amoore, which takes a theoretical perspective of globalisation and of Germany's capacity to sustain its socio-economic 'model'. Her view is that it is misleading to see the Anglo-Saxon model as a 'best practice' towards which all other 'models' will converge. The particular features of this 'best practice' are low labour costs and flexibility in labour markets – the two areas identified as weaknesses by Funk and Timmins. But the argument that there can be a 'best practice' model ignores the 'historical specificity and social and political agency of processes of social change'. Thus, the view that Germany is floundering takes into account neither the adaptability of Germany in the past nor the transferability of 'Anglo-American' structures into a German institutional context. Germany represents an *alternative* to the Anglo-American model where change takes place on an incremental and longer time-frame. Rather than being viewed as uncompetitive, this model should simply be regarded as different since it has shown its strengths in sustaining competitiveness in the past.

Marsh, in chapter 5, takes a pragmatic approach to the issues around German competitiveness and argues that the country is often praised and criticised for the same reasons. The institutions of the German 'model' are the source of the long-term incremental adaptiveness that is praised by many, but equally are at the route of many of the problems that the country faces. In particular, those problems manifest themselves in the profound need felt by the German electorate to see visible national and international achievements after unification. He argues that policy weaknesses after unification only served to undermine the consensus necessary if reform was to be effectively carried through. However, he goes on to maintain that Germany will not undergo a real crisis because of the embedded strengths of its institutions' incrementalism and inherent adaptiveness. There is, he points out, far more change taking place than may at first appear and it is this that will sustain the model.

Harding and Soskice (chapter 6) examine another pillar of the German model – the innovation system, regarded as the basis of the high quality, incrementally adaptive successes in German manufacturing through the 1970s and 1980s (Soskice 1996). This system has been roundly criticised as failing to adapt adequately to the challenges of an information and biotechnology age (Mason and Wagner 1999). But through a thorough examination both of policy and structures, they find similar evidence of dynamism to that highlighted in the chapter by Marsh. Institutions are at once inter-dependent and competitive. There is a high degree of networking and strategic partnership alongside real rivalry and contested markets. This *symbiotic tension* is the dynamic that drives sustained competitiveness.

Harding and Sorge (chapter 7) look at the final bastion of '*Modell Deutschland*' – its long-term 'corporatism' embodied in the laws that govern industrial relations and corporate decision-making. They describe the dynamic inter-connectivities between institutional actors (particularly education and training, industrial relations and finance) at a micro- and macro-organisational level. If a 'global' era is distinct then the important question is how these inter-connectivities and institutional rigidities can produce change. They examine the contention that it is the inherent incentive structures in institutions that generate this change. Commonly these are regarded as weak within German institutions and, hence, the system adapts only slowly. But, through an examination of emerging venture capital structures the chapter concludes that it is possible for a system to build in incentives without fundamentally altering its structures.

Whither Germany?

This is not a book about globalisation nor, indeed, a book about the current performance of the German economy. This is a book about Germany's future in a global era. Fundamentally this is about the capacity of its institutional structures to deal with change. The key features of the 'global paradigm' were summarised above as:

1 The importance of networks.
2 The centrality of technology.
3 The need for specialisation.
4 Swiftness to market.

Germany's social market economy is intrinsically networked and coordinated. Technology has always been central to German economic performance and its performance in the twenty-first century (measured through the technological component of exports) gives no evidence for suggesting anything to the contrary (Bertsch 1997). Its manufacturing and R&D indicators are heavily concentrated in the 'traditional' five sectors of chemicals, pharmaceuticals, electronics, engineering and automobiles (Belitz 1998; Cantwell and Harding 1998).

The issue, then, is the extent to which these institutions can provide the swiftness to market and speed in technological development that is the fourth feature of competitiveness in a global era. There is strong evidence that the biotechnology sector is developing rapidly and may, indeed, have over-taken performance in British biotechnology (Pfirrmann and Feldman 1998; Crowther *et al.* 1999). Equally compelling is the evidence that a dynamic entrepreneurial base is developing with individuals and financial institutions embarking on 'high risk' business start ups (*FT* 17 Feb. 2000). Specific regional policies, like the 'Bioregio' to stimulate biotechnology and the 'Innoregio' to stimulate innovation generally have complemented national structures like the developing INSTI network of small business support structures to promote entrepreneurial dynamism (Bundesministerium für Bildung und Forschung: BMBF 1999).

It could be argued that these policies are necessary but not alone sufficient to create a competitive future for the German 'model'. Indeed, any country wishing to create a climate whereby its indigenous companies can compete on global markets must have such policies in place. But the critical issue under discussion here is whether or not such policies change the institutions of Germany beyond recognition (i.e. Anglo-Saxon structures have been adopted) or whether they merely complement the historical inter-connectivities of the system. The complex interplay between policy and history is gathering pace in the German social market economy at the beginning of the twenty-first century. It is our purpose here to assess its progress and its future.

2

Economic reform of *Modell Deutschland*

Lothar Funk

Introduction

This chapter assesses the progress of the Schröder regime towards achieving its dual manifesto commitments of reducing unemployment and reforming the welfare systems. Such a focus is justified on three main grounds. First, the combination of high unemployment, an inflexible, generous and therefore costly welfare system and with high taxes is widely regarded as hindrances to more growth and employment. Second the low unemployment and the comparatively high standards of living of West Germans due to strong economic performance until the early 1970s were symbols of the *Wirtschaftswunder* of the post-war period. Any medium or long-term decline in these two key areas would suggest flaws in the 'German model'. But finally, and perhaps most significantly, these were clear targets against which Schröder wished the success of his Red–Green coalition to be measured.

Since his election, unemployment is still embarrassingly high, employment is only slightly increasing and growth prospects (2.4 per cent) for the year 2000 are lagging as compared to the USA (above 3 per cent) and the European Union as a whole (about 3 per cent). Progress towards structural reform is split: a tax reform at least in the right direction after the Keynesian demand management experiments of the first months in government, improvements of the public sector financial balance and a rapid expansion of goods exports since the second half of 1999 are the positive factors. A rise in disincentives for more profitable labour demand measured in hours due to new labour and social regulations is clearly more problematic if one takes into account that Germany's unemployment rate jumps to 15 per cent if those participating in government schemes or in early retirement are included.

What table 2.1 hides is that Germany has lagged behind its competitors in terms of growth and employment creation since the mid-1970s, and markedly so since 1990. As a result, commentators have increasingly diagnosed a reduction in Germany's institutional capacity to cope, without unwanted side-effects, with new economic circumstances arising from technological and structural change, European integration and globalisation.

Table 2.1 **Federal Republic of Germany: key forecast figures for Germany**

	1995	*1996*	*1997*	*1998*	*1999*	*2000*
Gross domestic product[a] (% change on the previous year)	1.7	0.8	1.5	2.2	1.3	2.4
Employment[b] (000s)	36 428	36 158	35 866	35 994	36 109	36 170
Unemployment (000s)	3 612	3 965	4 385	4 279	4 106	3 909
Unemployment rate[c] (%)	9.0	9.9	10.9	10.6	10.2	9.8
Unemployment[d] (000s)	3 198	3 498	3 907	3 710	3 542	3 345
Unemployment rate[e] (%)	8.1	8.8	9.8	9.4	8.9	8.5
Consumer prices[f] (% changes on the previous year)	1.7	1.4	1.9	0.9	0.9	1.1
Public-sector financial balance[g]						
(in DM billion)	−104.9	−121.2	−96.5	−53.7	−44.6	
(in % of nominal GDP	−3.0	−3.4	−2.6	−1.7	−1.4	−1.1
Balance of payments[h] (DM billion)	−27.2	−8.4	−2.4	−6.5	−22.0	3.0

Source: Federal Statistical Office; German Bundesbank; DIW calculations; 1999 and 2000.
Notes: [a] At 1995 prices. [b] Domestic employment (average of quarterly figures). [c] Unemployment as % of domestic employment (national definition). [d] According to the convention of ILO. [e] Unemployed as a % of employment (standardised definition). [f] Price index of the cost of living of all private households. [g] On national accounting definitions. 1995: excl. revenue of 5.6 billion from the takeover of the Deutsche Kreditbank; excl. the debts of the Treuhandanstalt (204.6 billion) and the East German housing sector (DM 28.5 billion) transferred to the Erblastentilgungsfonds. [h] On balance of payments definitions.

This chapter is an attempt to evaluate current policy in the light of the slow adaptability of the West German economic model (as was transferred to the eastern federal states after 1990). It assesses the current policy challenges which arise from inherent rigidities in the system. This system served Germany well in the 'golden age' of post-war prosperity and full employment up to the first oil price hike in 1973. Indeed, until unification the system continued to produce comparatively good economic performance. This chapter begins with a short description and explanation of the rise of the German economic model in the first few decades of the post-war period and then proceeds to analyse the sources of the difficulties in core institutions since then. From this it raises the key policy questions with which the Schröder government has to deal, the reform of now dysfunctional institutions.

It goes on to look at the policy initiatives and to provide an analysis of the policy. Whereas Chancellor Schröder (1999: 7–8) argues that '*Modell Deutschland* is not outdated', the central contention of this chapter is that the model contains institutional rigidities which prevent significant reductions in the level of unemployment and which have hampered growth since the end of the 'golden age'. Only coherent employment-friendly institutional reforms will solve the present and future problems of *Standort Deutschland*. Two pathways to improve competititiveness do exist: first, a general overhaul of the 'model' in order to achieve old strengths ('innovation and social justice') or, second, a shift to the Anglo-Saxon model, which is often demanded by mainstream economists and parts of German business.

The rise and decline of the German economic model

For many years since its famous *Wirtschaftswunder* in the 1950s and the 1960s the rest of the world has associated west Germany with remarkable prosperity and stability, providing high wage rates, low levels of inequality and a good employment performance. To summarise this in the words of Erhard, the legendary German Minister of Economic Affairs, 'Prosperity for all'. The secrets of success were seen in, first, a stability-oriented economic policy with respect to inflation, wages etc. (Giersch *et al.* 1992: 45–184), second, a strategy of developing export markets outside the domestic economy which allowed German companies to take advantage of scale economies, and, third, a reliance on comparatively high levels of human capital and skilled labour that created a comparative advantage in moderate-technology products in traditional industries with comparatively high-price products albeit with a competitive price–quality ratio. All these strategies were able to compensate for the small size of Germany's domestic market and proved very successful in the early post-war decades (Audretsch 1999: 276).

Since the 1980s, however, it has grown fashionable, not only for German market-oriented economists but also for international analysts, to view Germany in a much more critical light. Even before the economic strains of reunification, however, cracks were beginning to appear. In 1988, *The Economist* described the 1980s as a 'decade of economic underperformance' for west Germany. It was claimed that 'soon it may no longer seem outlandish, as it still does in 1988, to extrapolate the past and point to a Germany that is not merely static, but, by comparison with its European neighbours, sick' (*The Economist* 1988). Indeed, only recently the chief-economist of the European Central Bank, Otmar Issing, used the notion of Germany as the 'sick man in Europe' (Marsh 1999). International admiration represents, therefore, only one phase of the social market economy. A second and still enduring phase is encompassed within the claims of critics who state that the characteristics of the German model, after being modified in the political process, 'will prevent the system from surviving the current pressures brought on by the process of economic globalization' (Davis and Reich 1999: 226). Two immediate questions arise from this:

- First, which institutions made west Germany's performance in the post-war years look exceptional (see table 2.2) compared to other big European economies?
- Second, what explains the gradual decline of the German economic model since the mid-1970s?

Characteristic of the post-war German economic model is a gap between the vision and rhetoric of an 'ordoliberal Social Market Economy' developed mainly by the Freiburg school of economics and the political practice (Dyson 1999: 220) of a 'middle way' (Schmidt 1987) of *Modell Deutschland* which neglects important elements of the social market economy model. The latter served west Germany, however, well in the first three post-war decades because of the special conditions in this 'golden age' period. Since then Germany's ability to cope with new trends has deteriorated and, therefore, the model needs an overhaul. The following institutional analysis will show that a better adoption of the core principles of the ordoliberal social market economy vision especially in the fields of social and unemployment policy would have resulted in better performance since the 1980s.

Ordoliberal theory states that it is most important to delegate responsibility for specific tasks according to specific abilities. Each area of policy must assume responsibility for what it can do best or where it has the

Table 2.2 **Growth, unemployment and inflation in the post-war period**

	1950–61	*1961–73*	*1973–89*
A: Growth: average annual growth of real GDP (%)			
West Germany	7.7	4.4	2.1
Average of UK, France and Italy	4.6	4.5	2.4
B: Economy-wide productivity growth: average annual growth of real GDP per hour (%)			
West Germany	6.9	5.2	2.7
Average of UK, France and Italy	3.8	5.3	2.6
C: Unemployment: average annual rate (%)			
West Germany	4.6	0.8	5.0
Average of UK, France and Italy	3.8	3.2	7.9
D: Inflation rate: average annual growth of consumer price index (%)			
West Germany	1.9	3.5	3.6
Average of UK, France and Italy	4.2	4.9	10.6

Source: Carlin 1998: 26.

most direct influence. The optimal delegation, therefore, is characterised by ordoliberals as follows:

- *The state should be limited but strong.* Its proper business is to concern itself with the ordering principles for a market economy, to create the right conditions for effective competition (to lower inefficient monopoly rents) compatible with political liberalism and to ensure that its own policies are consistent. In particular, the state should keep its expenditure as a percentage of gross domestic product (GDP) to an efficient, i.e. relatively low, level. This means privatisation wherever possible and an autonomous social security system beyond the reach of politicians (Watrin 1999). Moreover, it should refrain from *ad hoc* intervention in response to lobbying by sectoral interests. Budgetary discipline is favoured also to support price stability and to prevent the crowding out of private investment. Demand side policies by the state are in most situations dismissed as counterproductive whereas supply-side measures can serve to promote growth and employment.
- *The central bank should be independent*: i.e. primarily responsible for keeping inflation down, but not responsible for employment. This is because otherwise politicians with short-term electoral interests might try to engineer a boom prior to an election, hoping that inflation

would not rise until after the elections, since monetary policy has a delayed effect on inflation. An independent central bank, therefore, is more likely to give priority to price stability than governments do. Hence it can deliver lower inflation and more stable growth as its policies are seen by financial markets as more credible. Sound monetary policy as a result (also) of central bank independence serves, therefore, to achieve economic stability (the West German success of the independent monetary policy of the *Bundesbank* in terms of inflation and unemployment can be seen in table 2.2).

- *Freedom in collective bargaining as a basic right:* one should keep in mind, however, that collective bargaining processes are the primary influences on labour costs (especially of wages) and working practices and, hence, have a decisive influence on labour market performance. Both sides of industry are thus responsible for achieving low unemployment and high levels of employment.

In practice and in contrast to the ordoliberal paradigm, however, the Bonn republic has only accepted the second and the third of these principles. In other fields the West German state supported a coordinated and proactive response to market forces within an institutional framework that can be characterised as 'corporatist', i.e. it was built on joint contributions of business, labour and the state. Surprisingly to many proponents of this more interventionist 'middle way' of *Modell Deutschland* the West German economic policy approach did not achieve, on average, a faster rate of GDP growth per capita than other European Union countries. Between 1961 and 1996 the real average growth rate was only 2.8 versus the EU average of 3.1 per cent. (Somers 1998: 321; Dyson and Featherstone 1999: 795). Also more sophisticated analyses integrating a number of different economic indicators show that west Germany's comparative economic performance was only average (Weßels 1999: 103). This relatively poor result can be explained by some fundamental regulatory inadequacies which cannot be fully compensated for by the often praised German strengths of 'long-termism', incremental innovation, the system of corporate governance etc., although the latter facts remain important explanatory factors for Germany's strong trade balance position (Owen Smith and Funk 1994: 499–527).

The scrutiny of the core institutions of the German economic model demonstrates that they improved the 'social capability' for catch-up as compared to other countries, notably Britain, in the early post-war period (Crafts 1999: 60). The key element in the German bargain in the 'golden age' is often interpreted as an agreement by workers to moderate their wage demands in order to permit employers to make larger investments which paid off in higher future consumption. Compliance with this bargain was ensured by social protections for labour, representation of workers in corporate boards, a coordinated free collective bargaining system, and the government's occasional intervention via concerted action measures. The overwhelming success of this model in which companies treated workers as important 'stakeholders' and in which banks had traditionally a larger and investment-enhancing role in the provision of capital for businesses than in other western countries resulted in both, high real wages for most employed and generous social protections (Hefeker 1998).

The social consensus in favour of this model which had effectively solved market failures and distributive conflicts up until then broke away because the preconditions for success of this approach to economic policy faded in the early 1970s, in particular the rapid post-war growth and the homogeneity of the labour force so important for rather egalitarian wage and social policies (Eichengreen and Iversen 1999). The resulting rather aggressive union activity in the late 1970s also signalled a breakdown in the consensus (Black 1998: 10). In the following West German 'slow growth' period (Carlin 1998: 31), the response to the different pressures on *Standort Deutschland* has taken several forms, including a redeployment of German export activity into ever higher-quality, higher-value added commodity production (Coates 2000: 241), more protective labour laws to compensate the losers and resistance to incrased labour market flexibility in particular by trade unions (Giersch *et al.* 1992: 185–255). Firms, by contrast, have begun to boost productivity (largely by shedding labour) due to rising rigidities and excessive labour costs and exercise the right of exit to find more profitable business locations.

Since these trend changes have started in the 1970s, most of the traditonal institutions that worked so well at the rise of the German model became more and more dysfunctional, i.e. harmful for employment and growth, but hard to change in the later years. Low adaptability implied the decline of *Modell Deutschland* as an international role model because of the rigidities inherent in its institutions. It is to these institutions that the discussion now turns.

Free collective bargaining

The list of indicators of dysfunction in the German labour market is long:

- negative employment growth throughout the 1990s;
- persistently high long-term unemployment of around 5 per cent of the workforce;
- considerable unused potential for job creation in the service sector;
- under-employment in the age group 50–64;
- substantial regional differences in employment rates, with high unemployment in the eastern states in particular (*European Industrial Relations Review:* EIRR 1999: 15).

The collective bargaining system is dysfunctional since trade unions use their power to demand relatively high real wage increases even if this hinders improvements in long-term unemployment (Knappe 1998; Schmieding 1999). In contrast to former times employers do not resist too strongly when employment becomes more expensive than justified by productivity growth and inflation in Germany. This is because they do not want to risk disruptive, and even more costly, strikes in the age of just-in-time delivery and as they have exit options, they shift abroad or towards labour-saving forms of production (Siebert 1999b: 250; Wolf 1999).

Moreover, although rising erosive tendencies of collective bargaining especially in the eastern *Länder* do exist, wage policy in Germany is still mainly characterised by so called 'solidaristic' policies of trade unions which have, traditionally, set effective wage floors and negotiated relative wage increases for workers of all skill levels, thereby producing a rigidity of the wage structure. The problem is that while this system pushes the wages for high-skilled/better-paid workers,

> to the acceptable frontier, the principles of solidarity in wage bargaining and parity in social insurance contributions push up labour costs for the less skilled further and further beyond their productivity ... eventually, particularly when faced with a downturn, enterprises shed massive amounts of low-skilled labour. However, with the social safety net raising the effective wage floor in line with average wages, the low skilled are unable to price themselves back into employment. (IMF 1999a: 7)

This means that the German unemployment problem can be explained by the interactions of exogenous shocks (like e.g. sharp oil price hikes in the 1970s and, of course, unification) with institutions that hamper labour market adjustment, especially the social security and tax systems.

The most pervasive current trend, however, is the new direction of sectoral structural change away from employment in manufacturing to service sector jobs. In contrast to the traditional manufacturing sector, jobs in service industries are, in terms of skills, productivity and pay, very uneven (McDonalds low paid vs. IT expert high paid employment). Therefore, Germany cannot easily cope with solving the unemployment problem, first, as long as the level and structure of wages remain rigid with respect to changes in labour markets and, second, as long as the system of unemployment support is linked to historical wages in sectors where employment declines (Paqué 1999).

The new structural change is particularly a problem for persons who lost their jobs in the manufacturing sector and will have to find employment in the service sector while being unqualified to get a high paid job. They are the core group of the long-term unemployed in Germany. Isolated expansionary demand policies cannot play the leading role in reducing such unemployment permanently. This new challenge implies also that an export boom due to a weak euro will not solve Germany's institutionally based problems. Instead, employment-inhibiting rigidities of existing institutions have to be removed at first, ideally parallel to a business cycle upswing, to achieve lasting employment gains, a reduction of unemployment and improved growth.

Finally, labour costs due to wage bargaining are only a part of the labour costs. A brief glance at comparative labour costs, as in table 2.3, illustrates this (Abraham 1999: 352–3). The table clarifies, besides the great differences even between European countries in labour costs, that the financing of the social insurance system is almost as important a cause of Germany's labour cost problem as direct wages. Due to the central role of labour costs for the employment situation policy proposals have to take this into account.

Welfare systems and taxes

Welfare systems are, then, in need of reform as the present system hurts both labour supply decisions, because persistent unemployment in Germany is also sustained by high out-of-work benefits, and labour demand, which is weakenend due to rising labour costs after shocks to the system induced by the social security procedures. As Schmieding (1999) argues,

> When wage costs reach excessive levels, jobs are destroyed. This hurts the social security system twice. Outlays rise with the number of unemployed, and, perhaps even worse, contributions decline as the number of tax-paying employees falls. Payroll taxes thus need to go up even further to keep benefits at their high level. This increases non-wage labour costs, since firms have to pay half of all payroll taxes. As a result, firms have had to dismiss ever increasing numbers of workers. Since the higher rates also cut into the

Table 2.3 **Labour costs in manufacturing in 1996 (Belgium = 100)**

	Labour costs	*Wage costs*	*Non-wage costs*	*Non-wage share (%)*
Germany	122.1	130.0	113.8	44.3
Switzerland	108.7	134.4	80.4	35.2
Belgium	100.0	100.0	100.0	47.6
Austria	95.7	92.5	99.3	49.4
Norway	95.7	128.9	59.3	29.5
Denmark	93.5	145.8	36.1	18.4
Netherlands	89.5	97.4	80.8	43.0
Luxembourg	88.7	120.0	54.3	29.2
Japan	80.7	90.8	69.6	41.0
France	74.2	77.0	71.1	45.7
Italy	69.4	66.2	72.9	50.1
US	68.0	93.6	39.9	28.0
Canada	63.9	89.7	35.5	26.5
Australia	63.5	89.2	35.3	26.0
UK	54.4	77.7	28.9	25.3
Ireland	54.2	77.1	28.9	25.4
Spain	51.0	52.6	46.6	35.0
Greece	34.1	39.3	28.5	39.8
Singapore	31.9	39.0	24.1	35.9
Taiwan	22.5	28.6	6.2	20.0
Portugal	20.6	21.7	17.5	37.0
Hong Kong	19.7	26.2	2.4	8.2
Mexico	5.8	7.0	2.4	15.0

Note: Wages are defined as the before tax wage earnings including social insurance payments of employees. Non-wage costs consist primarily of social insurance contributions paid by employers.
Source: Abraham 1999: 353.

> incomes of workers, who pay the other half of the payroll taxes, trade unions are inclined to use any temporary cyclical upswing to get higher wages to offset these losses … As long as the German government does not break this vicious circle, each German upswing is at risk of being stymied prematurely by excessive wage costs. Unemployment is likely to rise from cycle to cycle, as it has done since the early 1970s. (Schmieding 1999)

A particular problem is Germany's rapidly ageing population and the pressures this will place on the social insurance system. Demographic trends indicate that an increasing number of persons over 60 years of age must be supported by transfer payments raised from social-insurance contributions and other taxes paid by the declining number of active participants in the labour force. The public pension account will start to go into enduring deficits in about ten years time. Increased spending on health and long-term care for retirees will add to the burden (cf. Knappe *et al.* 1999). The present *challenge* is that taxes levied to pay for social security are one of the biggest barriers to job creation. There is no reason to suggest that this would not continue to be the case in the future.

In principle it would be possible to finance future social spending obligations by raising payroll taxes to whatever level was necessary. But these would need to be so high as to discourage work effort – leading to shifts into types of employment not subject to these taxes or into self-employment – and would cut deeply into working people's living standards for the remaining compulsory members. The existing unfunded pay-as-you go pension, health and long-term care systems need, therefore, reform to prevent the social security bill exploding in the next few decades. Moreover, given the future costs of the ageing population, the German economy cannot continue to support about more than 15 per cent of people of working age on unemployment transfers or other social assistance. As ageing and unemployment reduce social tax revenue and at the same time increase social spending, there is an overriding need to curb such spending through lowering the number of dependents by encouraging unemployed people to work or retirees to work longer. This would raise economic output and increase the tax base.

An important means to encourage people to work, to spur investment and to create new jobs, thus putting the economy on a higher growth path, would be a comprehensive tax reform in Germany where the public sector during most of Federal Chancellor Kohl's era accounted for around 50 per cent of the nation's GDP – a level widely regarded as hindering entrepreneurial and employees' incentives. Hence, fiscal consolidation should be pursued, and public debt burdens should be reduced. The effects, according to the German Economic Research Institutes would be welcome:

> Cuts in spending mean, sooner or later, lower tax contribution rates, and thus greater incentives to work and invest; in the medium term this leads to higher supply and demand in an economy. (DIW 2000)

Additionally, a simplification of the tax law including a restructuring of tax rates and the tax bases for both personal taxes and the business tax code is necessary. Special in-work benefits are also conceivable, for example, a reduction of the proportion of any earned income to be deducted from the supplementary welfare benefit limited to problem groups (cf. SVR 1999: No. 21). Such reforms would be extremely important in an age of increasing locational competition, when *Standorte*, i.e. business locations, have to lure or try to keep mobile capital and technological knowledge as competitors to other states. Less success in this competition means less capital, implying a lower labour productivity or a smaller increase of it. This policy result shrinks, however, the potential for wage and/or employment increases (cf. Siebert 1999b: 241–55). Significantly, in 1999 Germany has drawn less foreign direct investment than the Netherlands, a country one-fifth the size. This indicates that while the firms' reactions to a comparatively unfriendly policy to business 'is part of the solution for German companies, it is part of the problem for the German economy' (Schmieding 1999).

Financial system, Deutschland AG, capital formation and research and development

The financial system has long been criticised for having a bias toward providing debt capital to established companies in mature branches and not providing enough risk capital for start-ups and companies with rapid growth potential in new industries. However, as reaction to the growing need of financial opportunities for new technology based firms a new hi-tech stock market, the Neuer Markt was established in 1997 and seems promising (Audretsch 1999: 281).

The term *Deutschland AG*, or Germany Inc., arose from the closed system of cross-holdings that saw banks and insurers holding large stakes and board positions in the most diverse businesses that in turn resorted to banks for loans rather than going to the stock market. Moreover, high taxes of about 60 per cent discourage from selling the holdings, which hampers the transfer of capital from relatively low to relatively high value added uses. The human capital formation system, it is claimed, is too inflexible in reacting to changes in skills profile needs (for example, in updating curricula and training standards). Finally, the research system is criticised for being too weak in radical innovation, which is needed for the development of high-tech industries (Vitols 1997: 31–2)

The dilemma with the state

From the mid-1970s the state emerged as being rather fat and weak instead of being slim (limited) and strong, which is a vast contrast to the demand of the ordoliberal model. The German state is 'fat' because it spends and regulates too much and this is not conducive to employment and growth. Heavy regulations of labour, social insurance capital and product markets have hampered a major expansion of private-sector service employment, which could have compensated for job losses in manufacturing (cf. Scharpf 1998). Additionally, Germany is well known for the politically attractive but, in terms of fighting unemployment, rather inappropriate effort to limit labour force participation through early retirement and compulsory shorter working hours. This was supported not only by collective bargaining partners but also often by the state.

German federalism is notorious for the fact that the various levels of government try to influence each other's decisions, which often leads to harmful policy blockades. Growth is hampered by this 'cooperative' federalism and the principle of uniform living conditions because *Länder* (federal states) which succeed in expanding their tax base by attracting more business have to transfer a considerable share of their revenue increase to financially weaker states. This lowers the incentives for stronger and weaker states to strengthen their tax base by a better economic policy because both cannot gain much by this effort. Therefore, Germany probably faces the challenge of translating the existing strong checks and balances which hamper attempts at reform, in particular the interlocking federalist relationships and the frequent opposition in the *Bundesrat* (upper house), into a more flexible socio-economic and political order, if the current problems are to be solved now and in the future. This would imply a better division of responsibilities, more financial autonomy for the various levels of government and more incentives for a more growth oriented tax policy (Seidel and Vesper 1999: 28; Jeffery 1999). The resulting flexibility would lead to a more timely structural adjustment in response to structural change.

The challenges of today are very different to the times of the 'golden age'. The German institutions have, however, been quite resilient to the necessary institutional changes to cope with the current pressures in an efficient and fair way for the society as a whole. Will chancellor Schröder and his Red–Green coaliton change this?

Schröder's response: the key economic policy initiatives and assessment

A striking feature of the policy of the Red–Green government almost until the end of 1999 was the abundance of chaos, confusion and contradictions – precisely the opposite of the consistent and steady economic policy traditionally demanded by Walter Eucken, one of the leading proponents of the German ordoliberal Social Market Economy approach (cf. Eucken 1982: 18–131). Current proponents of such an approach – including a large majority of German economists – argue similarly that successful economic policy must be built on a consistent concept, i.e. it needs to be comprehensive and far sighted and therefore, helpful in stabilising expectations (SVR 1998). By contrast, the Red–Green government appears to be 'making it up as it goes along', zigzagging from one approach to another without a functioning compass (*The Economist* 2000: 19).

Maybe this viewpoint from the press is misleading. To examine this, we need to assess the key policy initiatives of the Schröder government towards the labour market, fiscal policy and the welfare system (pensions and health insurance). Chancellor Schröder and his regime have set themselves the ambitious goals of lowering unemployment, securing the long-term viability of the budget, improving incentives of the taxes and modernising the social systems in order to secure the long-term viability of the health and pension systems. All key policy initiatives will be introduced first and evaluated afterwards (OECD 1999a).

Description of key labour market initiatives

Here, the key policy initiative is an alliance for jobs, training and competitiveness. This *Bündnis für Arbeit, Ausbildung und Wettbewerbsfähigkeit* are round table talks of the government with the social partners, which were adopted in 1998 and are supplemented by a European employment pact since June 1999. The aim is to develop a joint strategy at the national and the European level to encourage employment. At the national level the alliance for jobs is meant to develop a new consensus over a wide range of topics bearing on the labour market, including wage developments, reducing overtime, more flexible opportunities for part time or early retirement, modernising the vocational system and the creation of a low wage sector. The European employment pact tries to share information about successful employment policies and to implement some 'peer' pressure among governments to compete in successfully improving the national unemployment situations. Partly as a result of the European employment pact, a greater emphasis on active labour market measures in the public sector and on short-term training places for young persons is an important element of the government's labour market strategy. Eligibility criteria have been significantly widened. Moreover, a number of single measures occurred: for example, the number of employees in an establishment needed to qualify employees for coverage by employment protection legislation was also lowered from ten to five, reversing the 1996 change of the former government. Additionally, sick pay, payable by the employer for the first six weeks of illness, was restored from 80 per cent to 100 per cent of previous earnings (minus overtime).

Description of key fiscal policy initiatives

After a slackening of the consolidatory stance of fiscal policy immediately following the election, the *Zukunftsprogramm 2000*[1] announced in mid-1999 and the *Steuerreform 2000*[2] from December 1999 aimed at reversing growing public debt and regaining room for fiscal-policy manoeuvre. There will be significant cuts in public spending which will combine with expected increases in tax revenues (from fiscal measures which have lowered corporation tax while broadening the tax base). The reduction of public deficits makes such a structural reform unavoidable due to the Maastricht treaty's public deficit criteria and because large revenues due to privatisation cannot be expected anymore. The reform comprises changes in many fields. The main components are:

- Consolidation of the federal budget 2000 through cuts in public expenditure (each ministry is to cut expenditure by 7.5 per cent).
- Medium-term public finance planning (aiming at a balanced budget).
- Family subsidies (increase in child benefits).
- Reform of the corporate and income tax systems (a decisive lowering of the rates from 2001). This includes local taxes and maximum corporation taxes at about 38 per cent from 2001. Similar breaks are planned for unincorporated firms, a majority of more than 80 per cent. To finance this, subsidies will be reduced and the tax base will be broadened, in particular by stricter depreciation rules. Distributed profits are taxed by the significantly higher income tax to a maximum rate of 51 per cent in 2000. Additional tax cuts were announced in December which are to come into force by the year 2005: by the time, *inter alia*, the initial and top rates of the income tax will be reduced to 15 per cent and 45 per cent).
- Ecological tax reform: In the coming four years the petrol tax will be increased by 0.06 DM per litre each year. The electricity tax will be increased by 0.05 DM per unit each year. The resulting tax revenue will be used to subsidise the contribution rates of the public pension system which is expected to fall from 19.5 per cent of gross wages in late 1999 to 18.5 per cent of gross wages in 2003.

- Zero tax on selling off cross-holdings, particularly of interest to banks and insurance companies who held shares previously subject to a rate of nearly 60 per cent.
- Pension reform. According to the German social insurance formula, pensions are index-linked to net wages. This formula is to be dropped for pension increases in 2000 and 2001 when only minor adjustments for inflation will be made.

Social policy initiatives

The government has cancelled former reforms aimed at lowering the future pension problems through the introduction of a demographic life-expectancy adjustment to the annual pension-adjustment formula and reforms to the invalidity pension schemes. Furthermore, the government has widened the contribution base to casual jobs with a pay of less than 630 DM per month and some of the self-employed. This will raise claims in the future. The new energy tax serves to reduce and stabilise the pension rate contribution rate. Further plans for a fundamental tax reform can be expected in 2001. One idea by a member of the government, a compulsory supplemental funded component needs to be developed further.

The key elements of the original health reform proposals in order to control costs of health expenditure were the imposition of a 'global budget', unification of hospital construction finance, a 'positive list' of prescribable drugs, closer coordination of the hospital and general practitioner sections of health services and measures to foster the grouping of doctors into clinics, including a much greater use of family doctors. For political reasons the first three proposals did not have a chance. Instead, sectoral budgets will be set and cost control introduced by holding individual practitioners liable for cost overruns (Economist Intelligence Unit 2000: 21).

Assessment of labour market initiatives

According to many commentators the first year was a lost year for fighting unemployment. There has been no real progress in reaching the goal of lowering unemployment. The main result of the several '*Spitzengespräche*' (or top level consultations) among the trade unions and leaders of employers' associations within the Alliance for Jobs were set-piece compromises which different actors interpret differently according to their self-interest and mutual blame-shifting for lack of adequate measures. The IMF sees the European employment pact as supplementary to national employment pacts and this assessment is probably correct. It 'seems unlikely to add sufficiently to pressures for meaningful and long overdue reforms' (IMF 1999: 21). What is worse, the measures taken up to early 2000 are not likely to facilitate better labour market performance, some of them are even counterproductive (e.g. higher sick pay).

Active employment measures in the new *Länder* had led to generally disappointing results (OECD 1999a: 19). The general bias in favour of strengthening corporatist institutions without more accountability for the actors is up until now no panacea. A more successful approach for the Alliance for Jobs round table talks could be to negotiate on an overall package instead of presenting proposals for singular topics. This would make it easier for all sides to give in in some fields as obvious success can be presented to their own supporters in other fields.

Assessment of fiscal policy initiatives

Reform aimed at structural change to reduce the budget deficit is necessary and long overdue, although some open questions remain in its present shape. For example, is the increasing difference of the tax rates on distributed profits and undistributed profits compatible with the constitution? The government's business tax reform – reducing seemingly high taxes while at the same time broadening the tax base – is a move towards a more neutral tax system, with a more internationally competitive tax rate. The reform package including the abolishment (or, after compromising probably, significant reduction) of the tax for selling cross-holdings is likely to have a positive effect on the expectations of investors and consumers. But even if a relatively bold tax reform stimulates growth and better incentives, employment growth will be low as long as the insiders in the labour market have the power to use the additional leeway of more growth for themselves to force through higher wages.

Assessment of key social policy initiatives

The financial limits of the current unfunded pension system have already been reached and there is no way of avoiding a rigorous reform through additional cover from private insurance funded through the capital markets, together with reductions in pensions levels. Therefore, the abolishment of the demographic life expectancy adjustment seems counterproductive from an economic point of view, because similar measures will be reintroduced again. Moreover, some proposals to make parts of the unfunded pensions more generous, seem problematic as well. The discussion about supplementary pensions is, however, fruitful, because this will clarify that an obligatory savings plan can be necessary to compensate for the lack of savings incentives of low income individuals. Due to the inclusion of casual jobs into compulsory pension insurance, the cost of business has risen and the Deutsche Bundesbank (1999: 32) reports that 'there is likely to be a significant fall in the number of hours worked'. This implies lower market incomes due to this regulation and a likely increase of employment in the black market. Finally, the new health reforms disregard under the overriding constraint of not increasing contribution rates the dynamics of the health care markets. Therefore, the reform 'could prove to have only a short run effect in terms of expenditure control' (OECD 1999: 17).

Concluding remarks: Germany at the crossroads?

Perpetual mass unemployment and chronic economic underperformance remain big problems because 'the political moves that have been made to date have been selective and, in part, even contradictory' (SVR 1999). Germany, which accounts for one-third of the euro-zone's economy, is and remains, in many ways a laggard now. Most smaller countries in the euro-zone, such as the Netherlands, Denmark and Ireland, are further ahead in restructuring and fighting unemployment. Although the centre-left government has announced further tax reductions and alterations to other institutional incentives, this is not consistently happening and, therefore, is not resulting in a decisive increase of growth or the employment content of it. The bulk of restructuring is being undertaken by the private sector, in mergers and rationalisations that are beginning to spread across frontiers. Largely thanks to the euro, this is being spurred on by a new dynamism in capital markets.

The other positive changes in Germany have been almost entirely confined to budgetary and fiscal policy, with the federal government adopting international standards in the legislative proposals of December 1999 to reform income and corporate taxation. In particular, more market-oriented labour market reforms are still rejected by the government. The mentioned measures and proposals still include almost no direct measures on loosening the country's notoriously rigid labour market, which features the longest vacations and costliest benefits in the world. In some respects, in the new millennium, the same old, outdated rituals and taboos persist in wage bargaining and labour-market policy as in the Bonn republic since the mid-1970s. The underlying problem is that the general institutional framework steering the incentives to work and labour demand is inappropriate to some degree for Germany (cf. Hasse

1999; Funk 1999). The institutional framework of the labour market emerged in times of high growth rates and high productivity growth and is even now being defended as a social entitlement by the still rather powerful trade unions, who disregard the fact that the global environment and structural change have altered dramatically.

Therefore, the reform efforts up until now alone – incomprehensible governmental reforms and private sector restructuring – will not in themselves solve Germany's unemployment and low growth problems. The non-institutional part of unemployment could be relatively quickly reduced by higher growth of output. A decisive increase in the employment-content of growth, however, needs more comprehensive institutional reforms. In both aspects, the new government was not very effective until the end of 1999. First, the expected small upswing and return of higher growth in the year 2000 is mainly due to factors beyond the control of individual governments in the euro-zone: low interest rates set by the European Central Bank and the expectation of a more or less neutral monetary policy in the following year, under-valuation of the euro against the dollar partially due to the growth and interest rate differential between the USA and mainland Europe and economic recovery in many of Europe's developing country export markets. Second, the economic policy practice of the new government has failed to stabilise expectations in its first year. This has weakened the economic climate and lowered the chances for employment creating investments. Third, far more than their competitors in Britain, the United States and the more successful European countries, Germany's companies have been forced by a combination of high taxes, high social charges and direct labour costs plus strong regulations – in particular a discouragement from hiring workers by laws that make it very difficult to fire them – to invest in machines rather than in employment.

Experience shows that a more comprehensive approach of institutional reforms is necessary than is adopted until now to lower enduringly the apparently perpetual mass unemployment problem, to increase employment and to improve competitiveness. As Germany is at a critical juncture at the start of the millennium, politicians have to act decisively along one of the following lines:

- Try to preserve and partly even strengthen the traditional institutional setup despite the contradictions involved, because existing innovative ideas cannot be forced through due to (apparent) political infeasibility. Such a resistance to change of the institutions of the old model Germany implies the introduction of protectionist and defensive measures which will result in low trend-growth and falling employment. This approach is very likely doomed economically (competitiveness shrinks because the old institutions are not compatible with new trends) and politically in the medium term due to the visibility of a better success of alternative political programmes.

- Simply accept whatever the markets deliver. Such a radical liberal market economy strategy seems neither politically feasible in Germany in the short term nor justified in terms of distribution or efficiency.
- Try to find ways to shape the future of the business location by strategic changes of the institutional setup within an offensive strategy to capture the economic gains while preserving social cohesion.

It is this last choice, the economics of an improved 'middle way' in a new economic environment which, arguably, presents the best, but equally the most challenging, route.

Notes

1 Programme for the Future 2000.

2 Tax Reform 2000.

3

Alliance for Jobs: labour market policy and industrial relations after the 1998 elections

Graham Timmins

Unemployment and the German model

Although unification has provided the focus of most academic attention in Germany during the 1990s, the structural difficulties of the German economy have remained a persistent underlying concern. For Helmut Kohl, the 'unity chancellor', his failure to tackle these difficulties prompted his electoral defeat in 1998 after 16 years in power. Soon after the SPD's election victory, the new chancellor, Gerhard Schröder, was clear where his main priority lay and stressed that, 'tackling high unemployment is the biggest challenge confronting the political system and society as a whole approaching the next century'. A higher rate of employment is not a utopian dream but a realistic objective, which through a focused combination of economic and political activities can be achieved gradually (Bundesministerium für Arbeit und Sozialordnung 1998: 1–2).

The policy response to unemployment has been a tripartite 'Alliance for Jobs' arrangement between the government, employers associations and trade unions designed to address structural tensions in the German labour market through a range of reform initiatives. As such, Alliance for Jobs represents a continuation of the post-war German tradition of seeking consensual solutions to economic difficulties. The development of Alliance for Jobs originated within the German labour movement following a proposal by Klaus Zwickel of the Metalworkers' Union, IG Metall, in 1995 before being taken up by Schröder during the 1998 election campaign. At the heart of the German economic debate is the extent to which consensus-seeking mechanisms are an appropriate response to the competitive pressures experienced by the German economy at the start of the twenty-first century. As will be seen below, Alliance for Jobs has yet to yield tangible results and there is some pessimism regarding the political will to succeed among the employers associations and unions. The argument in this chapter is that the evidence to date regarding the Alliance for

Jobs suggests a highly pessimistic scenario. However, the durability of the social partnership in Germany should not be underestimated. Despite the considerable tensions that currently exist, there is little indication that either social partner is willing to jeopardise the institutional framework of *Modell Deutschland.*

It is tempting to point to unification in 1990 as the catalyst for the present problems in the German labour market. In reality, German unity had the effect of exacerbating an existing problem that had been developing from the 1960s onwards. Having stood at just 149,000 in 1970, unemployment rose to 1 million in 1975 and by 1985 had increased to 2.3 million as global competition in the heavy industrial and manufacturing sectors increased. Unemployment declined gradually during the late 1980s and the immediate impact of unification was to reduce unemployment in the western states to 1.7 million in 1991. But by 1993 the combined unemployment figures in the western and eastern states hit 3 million and in 1997 the 4 million mark was reached for the first time. Since coming to power in September 1998, Germany's first Red–Green coalition has made little impact on the labour market short of a slight alleviation in the western states and deterioration in the eastern states. In net terms, however, the overall situation remained static (see table 3.1).

Table 3.1 **German labour market trends, October 1998–September 1999**

	Number (000s)	*(%)*	*West (%)*	*East (%)*	*Men (%)*	*Women (%)*	*Under 25 (%)*
Oct. 1998	3,892	10.1	8.7	15.7	10.5	12.0	10.8
Nov. 1998	3,946	10.2	8.8	15.9	10.7	12.0	10.8
Dec. 1998	4,197	10.9	9.3	17.4	11.8	12.4	11.4
Jan. 1999	4,455	11.5	9.7	18.9	12.8	12.8	12.1
Feb. 1999	4,465	11.6	9.7	19.1	12.9	12.7	12.3
Mar. 1999	4,288	11.1	9.3	18.4	12.2	12.5	11.3
Apr. 1999	4,145	10.7	9.0	17.8	11.5	12.3	10.2
May 1999	3,998	10.2	8.6	17.0	11.0	11.8	8.9
Jun. 1999	3,938	10.1	8.4	16.8	10.7	11.8	9.0
Jul. 1999	4,027	10.3	8.6	17.4	10.9	12.2	10.8
Aug. 1999	4,024	10.3	8.5	17.6	10.8	12.2	11.2
Sep. 1999	3,943	10.1	8.3	17.2	10.5	12.0	10.8

Source: Amtliche Nachrichten der Bundesanstalt für Arbeit.

The failure to address the issue of unemployment has led to widespread questioning surrounding the future viability of the German model or the social market economy, defined here as a 'synthesis of a free market economy, decentralised federal government and distributive social justice' (Goodhart, 1994: 7). The central concern raised by the critics of the social market economy is that the high premium placed on social consensus reduces the speed and scope of the German economy to adapt to global competition. Furthermore, the broader context of globalisation in many European states has been the proliferation of national stability pacts aimed at the reduction of unemployment and reform of the economy and welfare state as a means of maintaining economic competitiveness (Streeck 1998b; Hassel 1998). The result of this process has given rise to what Rhodes has termed *competitive corporatism*, i.e. a middle ground between neo-liberalism and societal corporatism which prioritises competitiveness, employment creation and redistribution but plays down the equity function of traditional corporatism (Rhodes 1997). Despite a long tradition of social partnership, Germany has experienced considerable difficulty in establishing a national stability pact of this kind. Streeck suggests two central reasons why this is the case:

- First, national stability pacts rely heavily upon a strong government line in coordinating incomes policy. The constitutional principle of collective wage bargaining independence in Germany has limited the extent to which the German governments have been able to determine an incomes policy.
- Second, there is a need for agreement between the state, government and employers on a long-term policy response to the economic situation. In this sense, the German pattern of social partnership is atypical in that it lacks the institutionalised mechanisms for dialogue found in other states typical of the Rhineland Model i.e. Austria, Switzerland, the Benelux states and Scandinavia (Streeck 1998a).

The main source of interest for the SPD government and the social partners has been corporatist-oriented reforms, such as programmes in the Netherlands, rather than liberal market reforms like those in the UK, although both have produced substantial labour market reform during the 1990s. There is little intention (or likelihood) of attempting a transplantation of the Dutch system into Germany since the 'Dutch economic miracle' has been predominantly achieved through the creation of part-time employment. However, interest in the manner in which the Netherlands has introduced a programme of painful reform through consensual means sends out a clear signal that few policy-makers in Germany are seriously considering the dismantling of the German model. The labour movement remains committed to the concept of social partnership and this is true too of employers despite the growing pressures for greater labour market flexibility and reductions in social welfare contributions and wage costs. As Silvia cogently describes,

> the single most important explanation for the endurance of the postwar German industrial order … is the degree to which core German employers still depend on it to achieve ends that otherwise would be exceedingly difficult to accomplish. [That is, (reliance)] on the rigidities of the labour relations regime to dampen domestic wage competition, to minimize labour strife, to promote and to standardize a high level of training, and to maintain a harmonious environment in the workplace. (Silvia, 1999: 115)

Referring back to Streeck's comments above, the main advantages of the Dutch reform process are generally perceived to have been the maintenance of political consensus and, more significantly, the centralised coordination of wage negotiations. There is, subsequently, some scepticism as to whether Germany can maintain the same degree of social solidarity and political consensus as in the Netherlands. As Davidson has argued,

> The smaller the country and the more equal the income distribution, the greater the chance for consensus and co-operation to support adjustment to a changing economic environment. In Germany, where the recent successful performance of the Dutch economy has attracted some attention, society has become more heterogeneous, and the income distribution more unequal since unification … Hence the co-operative model, which may have performed still satisfactorily in the former West Germany, has been seriously malfunctioning in united Germany. At present there is no indication that Germany would reach a social consensus about adjustments to fiscal, labour, and social policies as far-reaching as undertaken in the Netherlands in the course of the last 15 years … In our view, Germany will have no other choice but to move towards the more de-centralised and competitive Anglo-Saxon model suitable for larger economies. This implies further de-centralisation of the wage formation process; and across-the-board reduction of social benefits with less emphasis on the fine-tuning of instruments; and a cut in top income and corporate rather than specific tax relief designed to improve employment. (Davidson, 1997: 60–1)

In contrast to this somewhat bleak assessment of the future prospects for the German economy, two studies by Goodhart and Harding have undertaken investigations into the reform of the German model. Both are more optimistic in terms of the system's ability to adapt to changing economic and social conditions. Goodhart astutely points out that the contrast between the German and Anglo-Saxon models is not as great as many observers tend to suggest. The 'third way' strategy of the Blair government in the UK since 1997 has undoubtedly been influenced by the German experience in terms of 'economic management, industrial policy, social cohesion, welfare provision, regional government, proportional voting and, above all, education and training' (Goodhart 1994: 1) whilst elements of Schröder's *Politik der Neue Mitte* (Politics of the New Middle) suggests some attraction to policy transfer from the Anglo-Saxon model. Harding's assertion is that networks rather than markets are critical in our understanding of the durability manifested by the German model. In this sense, the role of social partnership i.e. cooperative industrial relations has been a critical in managing disruptions in the German economy throughout the post-war period and links in with Silvia's comment above (Harding, 1999a: 85; Hessel 1999; Turner 1998; Timmins 2000). As with Concerted Action in the 1960/70s and labour market intervention in the eastern states following unification in the early to mid-1990s, Alliance for Jobs, is another example of consensus-oriented crisis management.

Union–SPD relations after the 1998 election: a return to concerted action?

The election of the first SPD–Green government coalition in September 1998 provides the Deutscher Gewerkschaftsbund (DGB) (German Trade Union Federation) with only the second experience of a Social Democratic government in the history of the Federal Republic. Under successive CDU governments since 1982, the unions have been confronted with demands to accept more decentralised wage bargaining procedures, flexible working patterns and to show wage restraint as means of maintaining German competitiveness on international export markets. Taken together with reforms in social welfare provision, the unions found themselves frequently on the defensive and prompted accusations that the CDU–FDP coalition was seeking to dismantle the social-market economy. The labour movement was constrained in campaigning for an SPD victory in 1998 by its self-proclaimed position of political neutrality but did little to disguise its intentions in calling for a change in political direction. The upbeat response to the SPD's election victory and appointment of Walter Riester, previously Vice President of IG Metall, as Employment Minister likewise demonstrated union expectations that more 'union-friendly' economic and social policies would follow.

It comes as no surprise that Alliance for Jobs is the preferred option of the labour movement in that it perpetuates the inclusive practices of social partnership. However, the litmus test regarding the resilience of institutional arrangements is the extent to which they can accommodate pressures for change and produce results. If Alliance for Jobs is compared with the experience of Concerted Action in the 1960s and 1970s, the prospects for success appear less apparent.

Concerted Action was established in 1967 during the CDU–SPD 'Grand Coalition' alongside the introduction of the Growth and Stability Law (see Markovits 1986; Dorscht 1988). Under the direction of Karl Schiller, the SPD's Minister for Economic Affairs, an attempt was made to secure stable economic growth through Keynesian fiscal and economic policies. The so-called 'new economics' was aimed at controlling trade cycles, price inflation, incomes and unemployment through macroeconomic and financial planning. In return for union cooperation via their participation in the Concerted Action Initiative, a tripartite consultative committee comprising representation from the state and the social partners, the government promised to review provisions for co-determination within German industry. However, despite struggling along for a decade, Concerted Action never realised its full potential and collapsed amidst considerable acrimony between the SPD and unions in 1977.

The policy of social symmetry, pursued by Schiller in persuading the unions to moderate their wage demands, was a partial success in that growth rates increased to the highest level since the late 1950s but saw a rising structural disparity in incomes. It was, therefore, somewhat ironic that the September 1969 election, which brought Willy Brandt to power at the head of a social-democratic–liberal coalition, was accompanied by the so-called 'September strikes' in the steel industry. Having been initially reluctant to cooperate in the concerted action committee, IG Metall agreed to participate despite finding its position hard to justify to its rank and file. IG Metall and Gesamtmetall, having agreed relatively low wage increases of 4 per cent in 1968, union leaders were compelled to reopen negotiations in the course of 1969 as a consumer boom had provoked an incomes gap between the steel production and manufacturing sectors in favour of the latter. Employers in the steel production sector refused to accept the new wage agreement of 8 per cent negotiated between IG Metall and Gesamtmetall and in September 1969 a wildcat strike broke out at the Hoesch steelworks in Dortmund and provoked unofficial industrial action elsewhere. Spontaneous and uncoordinated industrial action is an obvious concern to employers but is equally a challenge to the organisational authority of the unions. At a time when unions are finding it increasingly difficult to recruit young, female, white-collar and part-time workers, few union leaders are unlikely to want to risk alienating the core membership with a repetition of the September strikes under the Schröder government.

The oil crisis of 1973 led to renewed tensions in the industrial relations system and came to a head with the first public sector strike in the history of the Federal Republic in 1974, a conflict that was to contribute to the resignation of Willy Brandt. Brandt's successor, Helmut Schmidt, inherited a fragile link with the unions. The public sector strike and the initial drafting of the Co-determination Act, together with the economic crisis, had stretched union–SPD relations to breaking point and came at a time when the BDA[1] had launched a propaganda offensive against what was perceived to the development of the 'union-state' as a result of the entanglement between the SPD and the unions. Schmidt's response to the economic crisis was an austerity programme that represented more FDP[2] than SPD[3] thinking and which the unions reluctantly agreed to go along with following the assurance of the implementation of a structural investment programme to address the rising level of unemployment and job insecurity. In 1977 the BDA took the Co-determination Act before the Constitutional Court in an attempt to have it rescinded. This was a move that heralded the most confrontational period in social partnership relations ever witnessed in the Federal Republic. The DGB withdrew from concerted action in retaliation (although the committee had long before ceased to be a forum of any meaningful cooperation between the unions and employers) in an escalating process of strikes and lockouts.

As Schroeder and Esser indicate there are numerous differences in the political and socio-economic contexts of Concerted Action and Alliance for Jobs, as shown in table 3.2. Most notable is the relationship between the state and the participating associations. Whereas the state had a clearly defined role in the Concerted Action process and both social partners enjoyed situations of relative stable organisational discipline, the state has a much less assertive role in Alliance for Jobs and the social partners are being confronted with considerable organisational tensions.

Whereas the fundamental objective of Concerted Action was to encourage the labour movement to accept moderate wage settlements in exchange for stable growth and generous welfare provision, Alliance for Jobs can be perceived as an attempt to lock employers into wage agreements as a means of maintaining social stability. The phenomenon of *Verbandsabstinenz* (abstinence from associations) experienced within

Table 3.2 **Comparison between Concerted Action and Alliance for Jobs**

	Concerted Action	*Alliance for Jobs*
Objectives	Achievement of full employment and tackle inflation	Address the various manifestations of the crisis of the social welfare state
Structure	Wide participation	Narrow participation
Political issues	Incomes policy	Various issues having direct and indirect impact on labour market policy
Context	National perspective, low unemployment, inflationary problems. stable social welfare system	Global perspective, high long-term unemployment, discussion surrounding future of social welfare system
Guiding economic and social policy perspectives	Keynesian approach – mediation of inflationary tensions through incomes policy	Supply-side politics and differential wage policy
Balance of negotiating power	State as guiding body for stable associations	State as moderator between associations

Source: Schroeder and Esser 1999: 11.

employers associations in the 1990s presents a real threat to the industrial relations system via the disintegration of independent collective wage bargaining procedures or *Tarifautonomie* (Schroeder and Burkhardt 1996). The problem facing the SPD–Green government is that it has very little to offer the employers in exchange for its cooperation other than the maintenance of social stability. Coming at a time when the neo-liberal agenda is exercising growing influence on the *Standortdebatte*, there is growing scepticism regarding the ability of social partnership to yield results (Berthold and Hank 1999). The government has even less to offer the unions. At a time when cut-backs in welfare state provision are high on the agenda, it is unclear what inducements can be offered to the unions to persuade them to stay at the negotiating table.

From the Chancellor Round to the Alliance for Jobs

Few believed Chancellor Kohl when he predicted first, that the eastern states would bloom within a relatively short period following unification and second that the transformation process would be a non-cost operation as far as West German tax-payers were concerned. Kohl had, however, demonstrated considerable political skill in selling East and West Germans a vision of unity which, although unrealistic, compared favourably with the dour (if more accurate) assessment provided by the SPD during the 1990 election campaign. Even during the 1994 campaign, Kohl was able to wrong-foot the SPD by suggesting that his predictions for the eastern states had been wrong only as far as the timing was concerned. The IG Metall strike in the eastern states in 1993 following Gesamtmetall's unilateral cancellation of the 1991 wage parity agreement together with the ÖTV's strike in the western states in 1992 suggested that industrial relations were entering a volatile phase. The response to the collapse of the East German labour market in 1991 was the establishment of *Beschäftigungsgesellschaften* (job creation schemes) as part of the *Aufschwung Ost* (Upswing East) programme. Nevertheless, the eastern situation together with the worsening economic situation in the western states prompted the unions to demand more pro-active labour market policies.

In June 1994 the DGB[4] announced its *Five-Way Strategy for More Employment* which formed the basis for the union position during the 'Chancellor Round', a social partnership framework established to discuss labour market conditions, in 1995. The Alliance for Jobs initiative was first introduced into public debate by Klaus Zwickel at the IG Metall Congress in November 1995. Zwickel offered the Kohl Government and Gesamtmetall a deal that would link union wage demands to the national inflation rate in the 1997 negotiations in return for a three-year no-redundancy agreement, an undertaking to create 110,000 new jobs and 5 per cent more apprenticeships. Encouraged by the successful introduction of the 35-hour week in 1995, Zwickel's concept was to link wage negotiations with labour market policy by using productivity gains to reduce unemployment levels (Löckener and Westphal 1996: 12–15; Zwickel 1996: 181–95). Discussions between IG Metall and Gesamtmetall began January 1996 but broke up after three rounds in March 1996 when it became clear that an agreement along these lines would not be reached. The concept of an Alliance for Jobs, nevertheless, remained in currency and was integrated into the Chancellor Round talks. The joint statement released after the chancellor round in January 1996 pledging to half the number of registered unemployed by the end of the decade provided some grounds for optimism that Alliance for Jobs would yield results (*Handelsblatt* 25 Jan. 1996). However, amidst the rhetoric, there was a realisation among all parties that little substantial progress had been made. Just days after the joint statement, the Head of the ÖTV, Herbert Mai, warned that the Alliance for Jobs was being launched at a time when large-scale redundancies in the public sector were being implemented. This comment tallied with the comments of the BDA President, Klaus Murmann, who had warned that expectations should not be set too high given the current economic conditions (*Handelsblatt* 31.01.96). The irony of the situation was that Alliance for Jobs was becoming to resemble less an attempt to create new jobs and more to save existing ones.

At the heart of the debate was the union demand for a reduction in overtime, which it was argued would go some way to creating new jobs. The government announced its Action Programme for Investment and Jobs at the end of January 1996. The unions and SPD rejected it immediately, however, arguing that the proposed intention to reduce wage costs had not been accompanied by structural initiatives. The BDI too announced that it was not fully happy with the government's action programme arguing that further tax cuts and a more radical reform of the social welfare system were needed if the government was to realise its intention of fostering growth and creating jobs (*Handelsblatt* 13.03.96). The Chancellor Round talks in February 1996 went some way to easing union concerns regarding compulsory redundancies with an agreement on early retirement schemes. However, the regional election results in Baden–Württemberg, Schleswig–Holstein and Rheinland–Pfalz in March 1996 signalled a recovery in the FDP's electoral prospects approaching the 1998 elections and reduced the prospect of a Red–Green coalition. The FDP had instigated the Action Programme for Investment and Jobs, which the Kohl Government interpreted as having received public support. The conclusion was that the unions could be marginalised from the political debate and that the Alliance for Jobs agenda had become an unnecessary diversion (Streeck 1999: 3). On 21 April 1996 the BDA and BDI released a joint statement calling for a more flexible labour market and, in particular, a reduction in wage costs and taxation levels but failed to respond to union calls for structural initiatives. The unions perceived the Kohl government to be backing the BDA/BDI position in the Chancellor Round on 24 April 1996 and subsequently withdrew from talks. The unions responded with a public campaign and in June 1996 hosted the largest demonstration in German post-war history when approximately 350,000 protesters descended on Bonn to support the Alliance for Jobs initiative.

If Alliance for Jobs failed to achieve any tangible goals prior to the elections in 1998, it at least served an important internal role of providing a new impetus for programmatic renewal within the trade union movement leading up to the passing of the Trade Union Federation's new Basic Programme in Dresden in 1996. Furthermore, by taking a more flexible approach towards talks with the government and employers associations, the unions have risen above their often dogmatic image in the media and have been revitalised as innovating socio-political actors (Hank 1996).

Alliance for Jobs: objectives and institutional framework

Unlike Concerted Action, which was driven forwards from within the Ministry for Economic Affairs, Alliance for Jobs is less influenced by macroeconomic policy thinking and more by a desire to introduce deregulatory initiatives whilst maintaining adequate social welfare protection. Seen as a post-Keynesian initiative, therefore, Alliance for Jobs represents an attempt to steer rather than intervene in the labour market by a promotion of best practice within the private sector. One consequence of this approach is that the participating actors have been allowed considerable scope to define the Alliance in terms of their own needs and agendas. Indeed, the lack of direction provided by the Chancellor's Office is perhaps the most central criticism that can be lodged against Alliance for Jobs. As Esser and Schroeder argue, the differing interpretations developed by the social partners provides the basis for a situation of 'antagonistic cooperation' This will only be reduced if the Alliance for Jobs succeeds first in reducing unemployment via enhanced competitiveness and second, produces scope for political exchange between the social partners. In other words, it will succeed only if the unions and employer associations are able to sell the Alliance to their memberships and enhance organisational discipline (Schroeder and Esser 1999: 5; Esser and Schroeder 1999). Unlike the Dutch Model, therefore, political consensus can be viewed as a product rather than a prerequisite of the Alliance for Jobs (see table 3.3).

The unions could be forgiven a feeling of optimism following the 1998 federal elections but the honeymoon period for the SPD and the Alliance for Jobs was short lived. One of the first policies implemented by the new government was the restoration of full employment protection and sick pay. Conducted outside of the Alliance framework and viewed as a sop to the unions, this first step did little to reassure the employer associations that the government would act in an even-handed manner and con-

Table 3.3 **Alliance for Jobs: objectives, preferences, taboos and references**

	Government	*Unions*	*Employers*
Main objective	Reduce unemployment and reduce public spending	Reduce unemployment and develop social-welfare state	Reduce costs and erode social-welfare state
Short-term policy preferences	Reduce youth unemployment and pension reform	Reduce youth unemployment and pension reform	Reduction in taxation and wage moderation
Taboo areas	Increase in public spending	Erosion of independent wage bargaining	
Reference	UK, France and Netherlands	Alliance concept from 1995	Netherlands

Source: Schroeder and Esser 1999: p.9.

tributed to the development of an antagonistic atmosphere. The general objectives for the Alliance for Jobs and guidelines for negotiation were set out at the initial round of talks on 7 December 1998. These were:

- a reduction in marginal wage costs and reform of the social insurance system;
- a more flexible labour market designed to reduce reliance on overtime;
- reform of corporate taxation system with specific attention paid to medium-sized enterprises;
- improvement in innovation and competitiveness of enterprises;
- flexible and improved provision of early pension schemes;
- wage negotiations that support creation of jobs;
- improved access to risk capital for small and medium-sized enterprises;
- improvement in savings and profit-sharing opportunities for employees;
- an ongoing dialogue concerning job creation, innovation and competitiveness;
- removal of structural obstacles for the creation and development of new enterprises;
- increased employment and training opportunities for semi-skilled employees;

- labour market policies designed specifically to address youth and long-term unemployment (Bundesministerium für Arbeit und Sozialordnung 1998: 1).

Similarities in the institutional arrangements between Concerted Action and Alliance for Jobs are inevitable. Both are tripartite arrangements and are based around peak-level negotiations. The institutional framework for the Alliance for Jobs comprise a steering group and benchmarking group under the leadership of the Chancellor's Office and nine working groups under the leadership of various ministries and, as such, are not too different to the structures established for Concerted Action (Dorscht 1988). What is clear from this framework is that Alliance for Jobs seeks to address the specific issue of unemployment within the context of a large number of socio-economic debates, the objective being to address the causes of long-term unemployment from an holistic perspective. As will be seen below, this ambitious project, reminiscent of Tony Blair's desire for 'joined-up government' has been complicated by the difficulties experienced in coordinating the work of the various ministries involved (see table 3.4).

Table 3.4 **The Alliance for Jobs committee structure**

Group	*Leadership*
Steering group	Chancellor's Office
Benchmarking group	Chancellor's Office
Training	Ministry for Training
Taxation	Ministry of Finance
Early retirement	Ministry of Labour
Pensions and unemployment benefit	Ministry of Labour
Working hours	Ministry of Labour
National and disability Insurance	Ministry of Health
Eastern reconstruction	Chancellor's Office
Severance pay	Ministry for Labour
Expert and thematic discussion	Ministry for Economic Affairs

The main forum for top-level discussion is convened under the leadership of the Chancellor comprising the Ministers for Financial Affairs, Economic Affairs, Labour, Health and the Chancellor's Office and Presidents of the Confederation of German Industries (BDI), The German Federation of Employers (BDA), The Association of German Chambers of Industry and Commerce (DIHT) and German Association of Wholesalers and Exporters, German Trade Union Federation (DGB), German Salaried Employees Union (DAG), Metalworkers Union (IG Metall), Chemical Workers Union (IGBCE) and the Public Service and Transport Workers union (ÖTV). The benchmarking committee consists mainly of academics and has the task of comparing the Alliance for Jobs with other international examples of concerted action as well as considering the broader political and socio-economic implications of the Alliance's work. As such, their inclusion is a distinct difference to Concerted Action format but stops short of the benchmarking committee's own aspiration for membership of the steering committee.

Alliance for Jobs and the Schröder government

By the time the second round of talks commenced on 25 February 1999, relations between the unions and employers had become more strained by a series of warning strikes. IG Metall had set the tone for the 1999 wage round by demanding a 6.5 per cent increase. The employers association, Gesamtmetall, responded with a counter offer of 2.3 per cent and talks broke down in early February 1999. Arbitration was agreed and IG Metall threatened to commence strike ballots if agreement was not reached by 17 February 1999. An arbitrated compromise of 3.2 per cent was agreed and two weeks later the largest public sector union, ÖTV agreed a 3.1 per cent increase. Dieter Hundt, Head of the BDA, argued that the IG Metall-Gesamtmetall arbitration process had been conducted in an 'oppressive' atmosphere and that 'an Alliance for Jobs has no point without a basic agreement on wage conditions' (*Handelsblatt* 19/20 Feb. 1999). Hundt's position represented the more moderate reaction compared to Hans-Peter Stihl of DIHT[5] and Hans-Olaf Henkel of the BDI[6] cast doubt on whether they would be inclined to continue participation in Alliance for Jobs talks under such circumstances.

The declaration released on 9 March 1999 at the end of the second round of talks provided support for regional initiatives and highlighted the need for more apprenticeships as a means of addressing youth unemployment. It was also agreed that arrangements for a more effective exchange of information would be implemented. This announcement is of interest not only in terms of relations between the social partners but between the various ministries involved in the Alliance for Jobs negotiations. The principle of ministerial autonomy (*Ressortsprinzip*) has proven an additional difficulty within the Alliance framework given the unwillingness of ministries to share information. Since it was contentious, the SPD and Greens agreed not to discuss the introduction of an ecological tax within the Alliance framework. Similarly, conflict within the government resulted in the Ministry of Labour insisting that the proposal to introduce social protection mechanisms for employees in low-wage occupations, the so-called 'DM 630 jobs', be conducted outside of the Alliance framework too.

At the heart of the problem has been the failure of the SPD fully to define the objectives and structure of Alliance for Jobs. Here, the role of the steering committee is a good example. The initial intention was that working groups would discuss the issues within their remit and pass their findings to the steering committee. The steering committee would then seek to reach agreement and pass proposals to the Chancellor's Office for confirmation and discussion at 'summit' meetings. But given that the working groups were controlled by the ministries, they have been unwilling to pass on information on many occasions and this has meant that both the steering committee and Chancellor's Office have been unaware of the outcomes of discussions.

Ironically, one justification that ministries have put forward for not sharing information has been the inability of Bodo Hombach to co-ordinate agreements. The main issue throughout this period remained whether or not wage conditions should be discussed as part of the Alliance for Jobs talks. Hans-Olaf Henkel has been the most vocal on the employers side arguing that they must. Herbert Mai, Head of ÖTV, and Hubertus Schmoldt of IG Bergbau, Chemie und Energie (IG BCE) have agreed in principle whilst Dieter Schulte, Head of the DGB, remains cautious. Whilst accepting that some linkage between Alliance for Jobs and wage conditions exist, Schulte has still to agree to wage conditions being on the agenda at the next round of talks scheduled for June 1999. Klaus Zwickel has made it clear that IG Metall would not be prepared to discuss wage issues and the most recent statement from IG Metall came via Jürgen Peters, Vice-President of IG Metall, who suggested that the employers associations were preparing to leave the Alliance for Jobs talks (Stern 14 April 1999). This statement led Wolfgang Schäuble, then Head of the Christian Democratic Union (CDU), to speculate as to whether an Alliance for Jobs was possible given union moderation in wage negotiations was the starting point for job creation initiatives (*Handelsblatt* 14 April 1999). Zwickel had accepted this basic principle in 1995 with the launch of the Alliance for Jobs initiative but no consensus on the definition of wage moderation has yet been reached.

The lack of direction in the Alliance for Jobs talks provoked speculation about the SPD's vision in tackling unemployment and about Schröder's personal commitment to the Alliance project. Moreover, a leaked report by Wolfgang Streeck and Rolf Heinze, two prominent members of the Benchmarking Group, to *der Spiegel* in May 1999 produced further controversy. The report focused specifically on the low-wage employment sector and suggested that a combination of progressive tax cuts and wage subsidy would be a means of creating employment opportunities. Both social partners gave the report a frosty reception and had this detrimental impact on the credibility of the benchmarking group. A central criticism was that whilst the proposal may appeal to a deregulated service sector, it would have little relevance to the industrial sector – the organisational stronghold of both the unions and employer associations. Having appeared to back the report, Schröder has since backed away and progress along the lines suggested by Streeck and Heinze is unlikely (Silvia 1999).

The third round of talks in on 6 July 1999 produced a degree of success in the guise of a joint declaration on employment. This committed employers to seek an increase in the number of apprenticeships available and to reduce overtime hours through a more flexible use of labour. The unions in turn agreed to discuss wage issues within the Alliance framework. Both social partners had ensured that there were sufficient escape hatches in their undertakings to render the declaration little more than symbolism. Silvia suggests, however, four reasons for the apparent progress that had been made:

- controversy surrounding the 1999 wage round had subsided;
- removal of the increasingly controversial Hombach's as chair of the steering committee;
- more personal involvement from Schröder reduced antagonisms between the social partners and ministries;
- both the DGB and BDA realised the need to produce evidence of tangible progress that would justify their continued participation in the negotiations (Silvia 1999).

During the latter part of 1999, the government, unions and employer associations have been locked in conflict over the issue of pensions reform and the Alliance for Jobs summit scheduled for autumn 1999 has been repeatedly postponed so that agreement, if any is to be forthcoming at all, is unlikely to be achieved until some time in 2000.

Alliance for Jobs: problems and prospects

Alliance for Jobs represents the widespread desire to continue the use of consensus-based socio-economic management tools. That said, Alliance for Jobs has been beset with repeated threats to quit the talks from both unions and employers. Although neither of the social partners would have anything to gain from leaving the negotiating table, the brinkmanship at play heightens the pressure on the Schröder government to achieve tangible progress. The central question, therefore, becomes whether Alliance for Jobs is an appropriate institutional arrangement to achieve the central objective of reducing unemployment whilst addressing the wider debate surrounding social welfare reform. The failure to reach agreement on pensions reform by December 1999 as planned has only increased speculation that it is not.

The Dutch experience during the 1990s suggests that the implementation of a national incomes policy is critical to the success of concertation thus the non-inclusion of wage discussions in the Alliance for Jobs framework is a real weakness. The assumption made is that the constitutional principle of *Tarifautonomie* will continue whilst Alliance for Jobs addresses structural issues affecting the labour market. It is unclear whether this arrangement will be successful, however. The immediate task confronting the Schröder Government is the need to reduce conflict between the social partners during the 2000 wage negations and to avoid industrial action.

Neither the unions nor employers associations currently see anything to be gained from the demise of the 'German model' of collectivism. However, neither seem willing to accept the necessary compromises that its continuation would require. The unions argue that employers have sufficient capacity to fund the creation of new jobs through reductions in overtime and early retirement schemes, especially if the unions agree to wage moderation and flexible working patterns. Employers deny this to be the case and, in response, argue that it would only be possible to create new jobs with a reduction in indirect wage and social costs. Interpreted as a dismantling of the social welfare state, unions remain unwilling to agree to such cuts. Failure to reach agreement on pensions at the end of 1999 demonstrates the stalemate towards which Alliance for Jobs is heading. The SPD was quick to adopt the symbolism of consensus represented by Alliance for Jobs during the election campaign in 1998. Having done so, Schröder may find that his political future is now dependent upon its success. The first year of Alliance for Jobs presents an inconsistent picture. Whilst the social partners have rarely demonstrated sufficient political will to ensure the success of Alliance for Jobs, it is unclear what alternative strategies exist if unemployment is to be addressed via a social partnership response. Seen in this light, it is not only the SPD that has invested considerable political capital in Alliance for Jobs. Failure could have far-reaching consequences not only for the Schröder government but for the German model as a whole.

Notes

1 Bund Deutscher Arbeitgeber (German Employers' Federation).
2 Freie Demokratische Partei (Free Democrats).
3 Social Democratic Party.
4 Deustcher Gewerkschaftsbund (German Trade Union Federation).
5 Deutscher Industrie- und Handelstag (Chambers of Commerce and Industry).
6 Bundesverband Deutscher Industrie (German Industrial Federation).

4

The tale of the hare and the tortoise: globalisation and the restructuring of the German model

Louise Amoore

Introduction

The concept of 'globalisation' presents an arresting image of rapid social change and embodies an essentialistic view of the restructuring of states, firms and societies. For states, this image declares the imperative of a process of restructuring of basic policies and institutions. For firms, globalisation is generally understood to intensify competition and create pressures for new models of production and work. For societies, the demand is for greater acceptance of the role of the 'self-regulating' market in organising areas of social life. In essence, the dominant understandings of globalisation and concomitant restructuring, particularly in the realms of production and work, have tended to reflect the deregulatory bias of Anglo-American social practices.

For the restructuring of the German social market model, the dominance of the Anglo-American one as 'best practice' poses particular problems. A series of political and corporate debates as to the competitiveness of state societies in a global era have pitched the British deregulatory approach to restructuring as outcompeting the 'high everything' German approach. In terms of academic debates, even critical scholars have begun to argue that the Anglo-American model prevails in a global era that favours neo-liberal solutions (Streeck 1997). In political terms, the 'reality' of globalisation is understood to pose challenges to the ideas and institutions of social democracy (Giddens 1998). In corporate arenas intensified global competition tends to be equated with the need for Anglo-American-style lean production and labour flexibility (Price Pritchett 1994). The triumph of this interpretation of 'globally derived' changes tends to translate into a neglect of alternative understandings of what globalisation and restructuring may constitute for states, firms, and societies.

The central argument of this chapter is that processes of globalisation and restructuring should be viewed as 'embedded' within specific state-societal contexts. From this perspective, the debates surrounding restructuring in the German case cannot simply be understood as a rejection of '*Modell Deutschland*' and a search for neo-liberal strategies. Rather, the restructuring of the German political economy must be understood as debated, negotiated and contested in the context of a 'known environment' of existing practices. Viewed in this way, global restructuring brings to mind the tale of the hare and the tortoise. The 'fast but fragile' rapidity of Anglo-American restructuring sets a pace that diverts attention away from the 'slower but stickier' German approach. In short, the equation that '*globalisation*' equals '*Anglo-American style restructuring*' constitutes an oversimplification that neglects the historical specificity and social and political agency of processes of social change.

Globalisation as 'process': the restructuring imperative

If there is one aspect of the contemporary preoccupation with all things 'global' that is categorically not 'new', it is the human desire to apply a 'grand concept' (Block 1990; Webster 1995) to a period of history and to the societies that dwell within it. Past eras have been variously categorised in terms of processes of 'industrialisation', 'modernisation' and 'democratisation' (see Kerr *et al.* 1962; Bell 1961). In contemporary times, knowledge of social change has tended to be equated with the grand concept of globalisation or the 'post-industrial society' (Giddens 1998). The concept itself, with the root 'global' and its use as an action-process verb form (-isation), appears to be imbued with 'a special meaning and social power' (Amoore *et al.* 1997: 181). Thus, globalisation is expressed most frequently as a 'process', and one in which economic and technological forces are greater than the social or political capacity to apprehend them (Ohmae 1996; Drucker 1986).

In this way, the concept of globalisation has become rather an overused and totalising label for multiple aspects of social, political and economic change (Jones 1995; Hirst and Thompson 1996; Boyer and Drache 1996). Indeed, it has been suggested that the concept should be abandoned to prevent its reification in political, academic and corporate debates. However, there is a central problem associated with simply 'forgetting globalisation'. Though the term may indeed have come into general usage as a rather 'empty' and vague concept, it has become 'filled' with meanings that have significant implications for political-economic and social life. Globalisation has become inextricably associated with a discourse of imperative restructuring so that the 'global era' is defined in terms of a need for states, firms and societies to restructure their basic institutions and practices around a 'neo-liberal' model of competitiveness. For states,[1] this restructuring has been variously described as shifts to the 'competition state' (Cerny 1990; Palan and Abbott 1996), the 'marketisation' of the state (Strange 1996), and the 'hollowing out' of the state (Jessop 1994). The emphasis here has been on the need for political policy agendas that actively create a competitive, low cost and 'firm friendly' location for 'footloose' industrial and financial capital. For firms, the restructuring prescriptions that have been most dominant in the globalisation discourse have called for the 'lean', 'flexible' and 'adaptable' organisation (see Womack *et al.* 1990). Such restructuring imperatives send similar messages to individuals and social groups. In the grip of globalisation, we are told, there is little alternative but to transform our working practices, our employment expectations, and our overall sense of security and stability (see Beck 1992).

In this way, the ambiguous and 'empty' concept of globalisation has been filled with a set of neo-liberal policy implications. Ideas as to the competitive state and the competitive firm emerge as symbols of efficiency, flexibility and leanness so that the boundaries between public management and private management appear blurred (see Cerny 1991). Academic analysis of globalisation and restructuring thus tends to focus either on the borrowing of private sector doctrines by the state (see Weiss 1998), or on the bargaining relationships developed between large firms and agencies of the state (see Stopford and Strange 1991). In both instances symbols of restructuring success in states and firms are selectively drawn into a model of 'best practice'. Throughout the 1990s, the 'best practice' for political and economic restructuring has turned on an axis of 'business focused' state subsidies and packages, flexible and low-cost labour, deregulated financial markets: in short, a state-sponsored promise of 'no strings attached' for business. In this way, in some quarters, globalisation is understood to represent a neo-liberal political 'project', driven by the interests of the US and UK governments in coalition with business and financial stakeholders. In the next section we explore how this project is manifested in the debates surrounding restructuring in production and work.

Globalisation as 'project': Anglo-American restructuring and the challenge for Germany

The idea that a UK–USA policy nexus of market efficacy, flexibility, and competition has achieved a hegemonic status in the international debates surrounding restructuring has been widely documented (Ruigrok and Van Tulder 1995; Overbeek 1990; Van der Pijl 1984). From this perspective, the Anglo-American vogue for deregulation and flexibility is understood as a kind of 'project', broadly defined. This is not to say that a clear and coherent transnational project is identifiable, but rather that key interacting dynamics combine to establish a restructuring 'ethos'. At the root of this ethos, the normative assertion that the market should be free from the distortions of political intervention leads to the belief that 'optimal market performance is dependent on this condition' (see Esping-Andersen 1994: 712). In the realms of production and work, embedded social institutions thus become synonymous with structural 'rigidities' that undermine the potential competitiveness of the labour market through disincentives to work and constraints on business management:

> today, OECD economies and societies are inadequately equipped … Policies and systems have made economies rigid and stalled the ability and even willingness to adapt. To realise the new potential gains, societies and economies must respond rapidly to new imperatives and move towards the future opportunities. To many, the change is wrenching. (OECD 1996)

This identification, within OECD policy recommendations, of 'rigid' social institutions with loss of competitiveness and opportunity, is also identifiable at the regional level in the European Commission's priorities of 'improving flexibility within enterprises and on the labour market by removing excessive rigidities resulting from regulation' (CEC 1993). The underlying logic of this approach to the relationship between regulatory social institutions and global competitiveness is outlined in table 4.1.

The construction of such a 'trade-off' between social institutions and competitiveness has significant consequences for '*Modell Deutschland*'. As Streeck (1997) has emphasised, the 'triumph' of the deregulatory and low-cost Anglo-American model has positioned neo-liberal restructuring practices as 'outcompeting' the 'high-cost/high-quality' practices of the German social market. The debates surrounding the restructuring of production and work in Britain and Germany are presented in international policy literature as, broadly speaking, the flexible employment-creating 'leader', versus the inflexible unemployment-creating 'laggard':

Table 4.1 **Social institutions and competitiveness in the Anglo-American model**

Regulatory institutions	*Perceived inefficiencies*
Collective bargaining	'Sticky' wages/ distorted wage structure
Minimum wage	Diminished allocative efficiency of the labour market Artificial inflation of the price of unskilled labour Disincentive to employer to hire/train
Organised and empowered trade unions	Insider power Wage push
Employment legislation and protection	Costly dismissals and subsequent inability of firm to adapt flexibly to fluctuations in global economy Exclusion of competition from external labour market
Workers' representation and participation in decision-making (co-determination)	Undermines firm's ability to adapt rapidly to fluctuations in markets
Unemployment benefits, social security, income protection Welfare programs	Redistribution takes place in a 'leaky bucket' (i.e., inefficient and costly) Disincentives to join the labour market Reduces intensity of job search Raises cost of labour Negative effects on savings and investment
Housing support, employer-based health insurance etc.	Reduces mobility of labour

Sources: Atkinson 1993; Esping-Andersen 1994; Blank 1994; Berger and Dore 1996.

> While Great Britain was to be feted – especially by the OECD – as the prototype of a European model of flexible labor market – and industrial relations, Germany represented the other extreme: traditional, inflexible structures, that have been labelled as Eurosclerosis. (Heise 1997)

Put simply, the Anglo-American restructuring dicta that have emerged out of orthodox views of globalisation are such that '*Modell Deutschland*' appears vulnerable and inflexible. The basic claim is that an inflexible labour market combined with high production costs renders the German political economy uncompetitive and liable to experience the 'exit' of firms seeking to circumvent regulations. With regard to the 'costs' debate, the British political economy of deregulated and low-cost labour is widely cited as outcompeting Germany on price. Many studies show labour costs in British manufacturing to be less than half those in Germany.[2] The high non-wage labour costs in the German political economy are tightly interwoven with embedded social institutions and, thus, are difficult to address without wider social negotiation.[3] In general, the German high-wage political economy with its quality value-added production focus is presented as outstripped by the wage-flexible price competitiveness of the Anglo-American political economies.

The German model of diversified quality production (Streeck 1992), which successfully sustained German competitiveness throughout the 1980s and early 1990s, is experiencing a questioning of its sustainability under the pressures of globalisation.[4] Increasingly there is a perception that German firms must compete for the first time on both axes of price and quality as the 'Lexus effect' takes hold and increases the pressure to add value in order to sustain the quality edge, whilst simultaneously keeping an eye on price.[5] Indeed, the 'Standort Deutschland' debate within Germany itself has pitched the performance of the country's political economy directly against Britain in terms of its attractiveness to foreign capital, both industrial and financial. This debate has tended to focus on companies leaving Germany to invest overseas, particularly, as in the case of BMW and Mercedes, where the production sites have been geared to the manufacture of high value-added automobiles in low-wage economies such as Eastern Europe and South America.[6] The shifts of German plants to overseas locations by such high profile companies as Bosch, Siemens, and BASF, for example, have been contrasted with the apparent attractiveness of Britain to foreign direct investment.[7]

Overall, then, a series of debates have positioned '*Modell Deutschland*' unfavourably *vis-à-vis* Anglo-Americanism. However, the perspective that sees Anglo-Americanism as the best-practice response to globalisation represents one particular view of the world. Undoubtedly, it has been this view that has dominated in debates as to what constitutes 'competitiveness' in a global era. However, there is a case for arguing that the 'globalist' world view has demonstrably underemphasised the role of embedded ideas, institutions and social practices in conditioning global social change. Indeed, we could argue that this view has stated precisely that such embedded institutions should be actively decoupled and transformed through a process of restructuring. There are two central problems with this perspective – the first analytical, and the second practical.

In terms of the analysis of globalisation and restructuring, the insights of broad schools of comparative political economy, institutionalism and 'national capitalisms' literature, have emphasised the alternatives to Anglo-American style practice.[8] From this perspective, the problem with assuming a convergence of all political economies around one form of Anglo-Americanism is that this ignores the evidence for diversity in forms of restructuring. Restructuring debates and policy changes are thus understood to be 'embedded' within a society and, hence, to be shaped by the institutions characteristic of that society. The salience of nation-state rooted institutions is argued to create divergence in the restructuring programmes of different states (Wever 1995; Vogel 1996; Casper 1998), firms (Zysman 1996; Sally 1994), and social groups (Boyer and Drache 1996). These perspectives engage with a wider social science debate surrounding the 'refraction' of restructuring activities through the prism of distinctive and 'rival' national capitalisms (Albert 1993; Berger and Dore 1996; Crouch and Streeck 1997). This alternative outlook on the world helps us to see that German state–society may attach meanings to globalisation that are fundamentally at odds with Anglo-American prescriptions.

In terms of actual practical issues of restructuring programmes, we can identify further problems with the idea that 'Anglo-Americana' should be emulated by other societies. First, there are many countries in the advanced industrialised world who not only provide few signs of policy convergence around the Anglo-American model, but also actively pursue alternative strategies with divergent emphases, often with the 'strings' of regulation on economic activity very much intact. Germany has been widely documented as a central example of just such an alternative (Albert 1993; Streeck 1997; Casper 1998; Berger and Dore 1996). Second, in the wake of the East Asian crises, the Anglo-American 'best practice' has itself begun to show its fragility and vulnerability. We are increasingly reminded, for example, that the very policies that attract foreign firms through a promise of 'no strings attached' make Britain 'as easy to exit as it is to enter' (*Observer*, 2 Aug. 1998). In this respect, approaches to restructuring under the pressures of globalisation appear to take on distinctive dynamics in specific state-societies. The feasibility and, indeed, desirability of policy emulation begins to look decidedly problematic.

In the light of such problems with the assumption of an Anglo-American best practice, it is argued here that there is a need to capture the historicity of social experiences of restructuring. Globalisation, viewed in this way, becomes interwoven with, and defined by, everyday human social practices.[9] It is proposed that when globalisation is viewed as 'practice', in terms of the ongoing generation of specific understandings and social contests, we uncover distinctive aspects of German restructuring that contrast with 'Anglo-American' style restructuring.

Globalisation as 'practice': the contested nature of restructuring

Questions of location

In its most orthodox form, globalisation is understood to create pressures that *cause* states, firms and societies to ask questions of their basic institutions and practices. These questions are assumed to centre around the competitiveness of the *location* provided by a particular political economy. However, when the broad 'globalisation-related' questions of a national political economy are explored, it becomes clear that the nature of these questions, and the meanings ascribed to 'location' are distinctive.[10] In the case of Britain, for example, questions of 'location' are defined in terms of cost competitiveness. Questions are raised with regard to how government policy can most effectively clear space for a competitive environment for foreign industrial and financial capital. On the one hand, the response to such questions has been to create the image of a 'hands-off' deregulated state attitude to foreign firms. This has been seen, for example, in terms of a deregulated industrial relations system which allows scope for the negotiation of single-union or no-union agreements by incoming firms. On the other hand, a new and 'legitimate' domain for state intervention has been created where the competition state may 'play the game' with subsidies, grants and tax breaks (see Palan and Abbott, 1996). This policy focus finds its distinctive roots in historical institutions and practices. Thus, understandings of global restructuring have tended to be linked to the promotion of Britain as a low-cost location for industrial investment, and a historically strong centre for financial capital in the City of London.

The location questions raised by the German political economy may, on the surface, appear to embody similar Anglo-American-style understandings. Germany has traditionally been understood to focus on the diversified quality production system underpinning the competitiveness of indigenous firms. This emphasis has undoubtedly been problematised by perceptions of intensified globalisation: manifested particularly in the emergence of the '*Standort Deutschland*' debate. However, the '*Standort*' debate is defined in terms of innovation, skills and productivity, and, as yet, has not embraced the low-cost ethos of the British location debate.[11]

A reduction of costs in the German case would imply a radical restructuring of industrial bargaining arrangements, employment regulations, and the business tax system. Such radical restructuring is relatively 'high risk' in a political economy that builds its export quality on foundations of industrial consensus. Indeed, it can be demonstrated that the cost problem in Germany has been overstated. Despite the financial crises in East Asia and Russia, Germany continues to boast a current account surplus that reflects its export strength (OECD 1999). Though wage rises for the whole economy are set to increase 3 per cent by 2000, this is counterbalanced by improving productivity levels (OECD 1999). Business lending by the German banking sector continues to rise, reinforcing traditional German strengths in 'incremental innovation' (Carlin and Soskice 1997: 73). In this sense, the '*Standort*' itself is understood in a manner that reflects and embodies historical German strengths. Whilst Britain asks location questions that centre around 'how can we attract inward investment capital?', Germany asks 'how do we sustain a competitive location for our firms?'. Though we may consider these to be questions driven by globalisation, the meanings constructed are entirely distinctive to each country.

It is not only the case that different political economies generate divergent understandings of the location implications of globalisation. Within these distinctive interpretations of 'location' there are also a series of specific tensions and contradictions that become associated with the damaging 'effects' of globalisation. A central tension in British debates, for example, is that the pursuit of 'cost competitiveness' as a priority tends to lock a political economy into a kind of 'race to the bottom'.[12] The adoption of low-cost strategies, and the rejection of high-skills alternatives, positions Britain in competition with less developed economies and, thus, makes the British political economy vulnerable to company 'exit' (see Watson and Hay 1998). In short, the dominance of the foreign direct investment-oriented location questions has restricted the scope for alternative questions. In the German context, the dominant tensions tend to surround the restrictions on the availability of 'risk' capital, and related constraints on the potential for job growth through 'new' economic sectors. In this respect, the '*Standort*' debate reflects a relatively small, and diminishing, group of interests in traditional manufacturing strongholds, and excludes a larger group of, for example, women workers and workers in non-traditional sectors.

The 'time-frame' of restructuring

In a generic sense, the political debates surrounding globalisation tend to place their emphasis on the imperative of a 'rapid response'. This is manifested at many levels, from the state, where it is equated with a need for new 'third way' policy agendas (see Giddens 1998), through firms, where it is believed that responses to changes in global markets must be instantaneous, to societies, where the 'flexible' individual is lauded as a global 'player'. In some political economies this image of the rapid time-frame of global restructuring is particularly evident. In the British political economy, this 'instantaneous' conception of time reflects an overall emphasis on the equity financing of ventures and the consequent need to secure rapid short-term returns on investment in a 'share-owning democracy' (Graham 1997: 126). Within such a time-frame, the uncertainties of globalisation are exacerbated by acute exposure to the vacillations of world markets so that, for example, the collapse of the global semi-conductor market or shocks in the world financial system can be felt almost instantaneously at the national level. Thus, the nature of restructuring in Britain tends to be 'fast but fragile', involving few social groups in consultation and focusing on the short-term management of change.

The German restructuring focus, by contrast, embodies a longer-term view of the time-scale of restructuring. This protracted time-frame has, for many, been at the root of the problems faced by '*Modell Deutschland*' in a global era. However, the institutions and practices that underpin this time-frame have also long been credited with sustaining Germany's competitive success in global markets. The embedded system of bank-based credit financing for industries tends to privilege risk minimisation, giving priority to sustained stability and continuity.[13] Similarly, the formalised legal frameworks constraining and directing collective bargaining impose constraints on pay flexibility, yet are widely attributed with a role in maintaining consensus and cooperation in the workplace. The involvement of a wider set of social groups in restructuring debates thus favours a 'slow but sticky'[14] approach. The need for consensus protracts the contestation of social changes but ensures a wider acceptance in the longer term. This is not to say, then, that the German political economy is 'ignoring' or 'resisting' globalisation. Rather, the pressures of globalisation are attributed with a distinctive set of social and political meanings. The question, then, is whether an alternative 'slower but stickier' time-frame may create its own opportunities within the embedded constraints.

The 'social arena' of restructuring

The forces of globalisation are most commonly perceived to have *direct* effect on states and firms, with states devolving authority to markets and agencies through deregulatory policies. In this formulation, societies 'receive' changes *indirectly* through changes in political and economic policies for a global era. Within individual nation-states, however, processes of restructuring have taken place within the context of particular social arenas. More specifically, the tensions and social contests that have emerged out of restructuring have occupied distinctive social arenas in different countries.

In Britain, the restructuring of production and work has been actively devolved by the state to the level of the workplace. The policy agendas of successive governments have actively cleared space for private managers to exercise freedom in restructuring decisions. Whilst the British state has actively involved itself in the creation and reproduction of a 'low cost' and deregulated competitive political economy, it has tended to remove itself from responsibility for many of the tensions that have emerged as a result. In these instances, responsibility is abdicated to the 'dictates of global markets'[15] and the image of a 'powerless state' is reinforced (see Weiss 1998). Thus, the contradictions of the British restructuring programme have tended to be felt most keenly in the branch-plant workplaces where insecurity and uncertainty are intensified (see Rubery 1993: 17; Seccombe 1999), and within 'host' regions, where dependency on incoming plants may be acute. This has led some scholars to question the sustainability of the Anglo-American practices exemplified by the British political economy (see Watson and Hay 1998).

The German restructuring debate, by contrast, has been characterised by a series of contests and negotiations between the government, industries, and trade unions. For example, a central issue in the recent jobs alliance talks has been the question of early retirement. This is clearly a thorny issue. For the government, there are considerable implications for the costs of full pensions for those under 60. For the employers, the issue of labour costs is tightly interwoven with the debate. For the unions, policies of early retirement are crucial for job creation in Germany. A tentative deal was finally reached in October 1999, enabling employees to retire at 60 on a full pension, with the cost to the state subsidised by employer and employee contributions (EIRR 310, 1997: 7). The issue continues to be fiercely debated, demonstrating that the responsibility for restructuring does not rest solely with the firm in Germany.

A further instance of negotiated restructuring can be seen in the government's 1996 decision to reduce the cost burden on employers through a 20 per cent reduction in sickness entitlement. This policy met with resistance from trade unions and led to a process of negotiation between the unions and the employers' organisations:

> The deal seems to have satisfied the honour of both sides – unions have been able to maintain sick pay levels of 100 per cent of normal pay, whilst employers have been able to keep down the cost of the deal. (EIRR 276, 1997: 7)

The employers effectively agreed to 'trade' compensation for the government's cut in statutory long-term sick pay for a commitment to wage restraint in the 1997/98 bargaining round. By the end of 1998, 752 collective agreements had been completed dealing with sick pay. Of these, 556 provided for a full payment of 100 per cent of earnings from the first day of sickness (EIRR 305, 1999: 19). Here, the paradoxical situation arises whereby a government puts measures in place to reduce the employers' statutory contributions burden and the employers reject this in favour of maintaining continuity and stability. Similarly, measures to increase pay and working time flexibility have been implemented, but these have taken the form of 'corridors' or 'accounts' that allow for marginal fluctuation within established parameters. The restructuring of production and work within firms, then, is tentative, and follows the spirit of past practices.

We can see, therefore that globalisation does not simply cause a convergence of policies and practices around Anglo-Americanism. Rather, it is contested in terms of meanings and understandings, in terms of 'right' responses, and in terms of actual social practices in the workplace. The contests that emerge from processes of restructuring are imbued with the social characteristics of a particular political economy. In Germany, from a peak of unemployment in 1997, social contests have tended to coalesce around divisions between 'insiders' and 'outsiders'.[16] The insiders tend to be employed in traditional sectors with secure contracts and generous social insurance provision. The interests of these groups tend to be reflected in the bargains struck in the process of restructuring. The 1999 agreement between IG Metall and Volkswagen, for example, secured 3.2 per cent pay increases, but failed to obtain permanent status for the 6,000 workers employed on fixed-term contracts (EIRR 305, 1999: 6). An increasing number of 'outsiders', either unemployed, working in the 'invisible' economy, or on fixed-term contracts, are excluded from the benefits of German-style 'restructuring within limits'. Mahnkopf identifies a further division between the interests of a nationally rooted '*Arbeitsgesellschaft*' or working society, and those of an increasingly globally oriented '*Gesellschaft der Geldvermögensbesitzer*' or wealth-owning society' (1999: 159–60). From this perspective, key financial and productive interests can 'exit' Germany with relative ease, whilst labour groups remain relatively territorially bound. In particular, the large German banks have expanded their interests in the City of London, and multinational corporations have invested in overseas locations. These examples show how restructuring may be contested at several levels, with potential contradictions and tensions between the levels.

The contests surrounding restructuring in the Anglo-American political economies tend to have had the advantage of a lower profile than the ubiquitous 'problems with *Modell Deutschland*'. It is worth reflecting, however, that the Anglo-American 'model' is itself defined by a series of contests and social conflicts. Britain, for example, has experienced problems with long-term loss of skills and productivity, a trend exacerbated by 'flexibility' policies (Rubery 1993; Crouch 1997; Coates 1999). The loss of foreign direct investment over recent years has further reinforced the impression that Britain is indeed following a 'fragile' course of restructuring. Watson and Hay (1998) suggest that the 'hypermobility' of incoming firms may be overtly emphasised to exert increased pressure on the 'FDI-inviter' countries. Such pressure can be seen, for example, in the negotiations between BMW and the British government over the Rover Longbridge plant. In this instance a distinctive set of tensions has emerged between political and corporate interests, and labour groups. In Anglo-American 'FDI-inviter' countries there tend to be opportunities for the 'symbolic analysts' (Reich 1991) whose job it is to produce and manage information, and, in particular, for agencies created to attract and manage investment. These opportunities, however, impose simultaneous constraints on the life-chances of other social groups.

Concluding remarks

The contemporary vogue of connecting all restructuring in states, firms and societies to an Anglo-American defined response to globalisation has significant implications for social models of production and work that have historically been viewed as 'alternatives'. In the deterministic readings of globalisation as 'process', the 'logic' of Anglo-Americanism exerts particular force on the structures and institutions of '*Modell Deutschland*'. The dilemmas facing the German state, industries and society under the pressures of globalisation have been described as a choice between 'the devil and the deep blue sea' (Mahnkopf 1999: 171). This stark choice implies a potentially high-risk strategy of restructuring the diversified quality production model that has for so long underpinned German success. However, the suggestion that there may be a 'choice', albeit a stark one, gives some indication of the political and social forces that may inform that choice. Viewed in this way, the German political economy is not simply pressurised by globalisation into accepting the imperatives of Anglo-American practices. Rather, processes of restructuring are debated and contested in the context of a known environment of ideas, institutions and practices.

The emerging German patterns of restructuring, when made 'visible' in globalisation debates, open up alternatives to the assumptions and prescriptions of 'Anglo-Americana'. In a sense, the divergent 'Anglo-Saxon' and 'Rhineland' (Albert 1993) restructuring debates bring to mind the fable of the hare and the tortoise. The ideas of the Anglo-American model, like the hare, set out at a furious pace and, to an extent, defined the terms of a 'global restructuring race'. In this sense, the direction, speed, and nature of responses to globalisation have been determined by the experiences of a relatively small, but nonetheless powerful, group of interests. The strengths of the tortoise, more characteristic of the German 'slow but sticky' restructuring practices, have tended to be less visible but, potentially, offer an innovative alternative of 'progressive competitiveness' (Mahnkopf 1999). Thus, there can be no single determining force of globalisation and no single 'best practice' route to competitive restructuring. Rather, many diverse understandings and experiences of the implications of global restructuring emerge within the context of specific state-societies. For the German political economy, the 'rules' in the global restructuring race may, indeed, be very different from those set down by the dicta of 'Anglo-Americana'.

Notes

1 The 'imperative' interpretation of restructuring under globalisation is embodied, for example, in international policy literature that seeks to communicate 'best practice' restructuring to individual nation states: 'The forces of globalisation increase both the benefits of good policies and the costs of failure … Whether a new golden age arrives for all depends mostly on the responses of individual countries to the new opportunities offered by this increasingly global economy' (World Bank 1995: 54).

2 The Bank of International Settlements (BIS) calculate costs in the UK manu-

facturing sector for 1995 at 45 per cent of costs in the same sector in Germany (*Independent*, 13 June 1996). Taking the United States as the index at 100, Freeman (1994: 31) calculates hourly wages of workers for the whole of the economy in 1992, at 91 per cent for the United Kingdom, and at 160 per cent for Germany. It is also revealing to look at the labour costs for two plants in the same company, one in Britain, the other in Germany. Osram, a subsidiary of Siemens, calculates that costs of employment (including wages, employment taxes, and related costs paid by the employer), are 66 per cent lower in its Manchester plant in the United Kingdom than in its Augsburg plant in southern Germany (*Financial Times*, March 1997).

3 Institut der Deutschen Wirtschaft (1997) calculates that the non-wage costs alone paid by German industry are the same as the total labour costs in Britain. Indexing Germany at 100, they show Germany's remuneration costs for hourly labour as 55, while non-wage costs account for 45. Britain's total labour costs are calculated at 45, 73 per cent of which is remuneration, while 27 per cent is non-wage costs.

4 As Streeck argues, 'a possible secular exhaustion of its capacity to perform the complicated balancing acts required for its success' (1997: 247). See also, Zumwinkle (1995).

5 In the year the Lexus car was launched, one model alone sold more in the United States than all the models of Mercedes combined. For further analysis see Hancké (1997).

6 Hancké's study of the restructuring of the automobile industry cites wage differentials as the principal incentive in the establishment of greenfield plants in South America by Mercedes and BMW. Both plats were established to produce high-quality niche vehicles – the BMW roadster Z3 and the four-wheel-drive Mercedes (1997: 22).

7 The German metal industry employer's association, Gesamtmetall, expresses concern at the levels of overseas investment undertaken by German metal and electrical engineering firms between 1990 and 1995, in its 1997 report, '*Bericht der Geschäftsfuhrung des Gesamtverbandes der metallindustriellen Arbeitgeberverbande*', 1 May 1995–30 April 1997: 25.

8 The 'embeddedness' approaches draw upon a diverse array of traditions, to include Polanyian insights (see Hollingsworth and Boyer 1997) and comparative political economy, broadly defined (see Crouch and Streeck 1997).

9 Germain's (1997) paper 'Historical Perspectives on Globalisation and Internationalisation: A Prolegomena', prepared for the IPEG annual workshop on 'The Globalisation versus Internationalisation Debate', emphasises the importance of an understanding of globalisation as social practice, University of Leeds, 8 February. Matt Davies' 'The Global Political Economy is Ordinary: Power, Production, Culture', presented at BISA, 15–17 December 1997, University of Leeds, similarly emphasises globalisation as lived experience and the inherited practices of everyday life.

10 For analysis of the British social system of production see, for example, Rubery (1993). For analysis of the German social system of production see, for example, Herrigel (1994).

11 Mahnkopf argues, for example, that in the German globalisation debate an alternative to 'cost-cutting' competition is found in 'innovation competition' (1999: 149).

12 The phrase 'race to the bottom' has become common currency in studies in international political economy. Its origin is difficult to determine, though in this instance it is used following the insights of discussions with Dr Barry Gills.

13 Albert (1993) contrasts the Anglo-Saxon shareholders value of equity financing with the German stakeholders value of bank credit-based financing.

14 I owe this point to discussions with Professor Wolfgang Streeck, though the usual disclaimers apply and I take responsibility for its presentation in this context.

15 On visiting the stricken Fujitsu plant in northeast England, Prime Minister Tony Blair declared that the British government could do little 'about the twists and turns of world markets in an increasingly globalised economy'.

16 The German economy is experiencing a widening of pay differentials. The trend is for highly paid workers to gain greater increases in bargaining rounds than their lesser-paid counterparts. In addition, agreed clauses have been built into sectors such as construction and smaller enterprises, particularly in the East. These clauses allow for 'pay corridors' of 10 per cent pay reduction when demand is low or other conditions are unfavourable.

5

A pattern of light and shade for the German economy

David Marsh

Introduction

Europe's most important economy faces grave problems, but their causes and effects have been much misunderstood – sometimes gratuitously and deliberately – by observers in Germany and abroad. Rather like former Chancellor Helmut Kohl, who was under-estimated by many domestic and foreign commentators for the first eight years of his chancellorship and over-estimated in the second eight years, the German economy is often both praised and criticised for the wrong reasons. In the throes of an immense period of transition, the German economy throws up a complex pattern of light and shade.

The German economy faces challenges on many fronts. The phenomenon of globalisation could potentially hit Germany harder than any other European nation, in view of its relative openness to foreign trade and the physical closeness of cheaper production sites in the reforming ex-communist states of central and eastern Europe. Even though unification in 1990 was a great and positive achievement, the effects of faulty economic policies in the initial years now linger on. The problems of eastern Germany perhaps reflect the last vengeful stir of Erich Honecker, the former East German leader, twisting in the grave of Marxism. But they also are partly due to the past mistakes of the West German government. Kohl's thesis in 1990 was that East and West Germany would quickly have the same living standards, and that the cost to tax-payers in the west would be insignificant. The probability that even one of these statements would be true was slight; the chance that they would both be proved correct at the same time was infinitesimal.

There is not just the problem of the drain on the German exchequer caused by continued large grants and subsidies to the so-called 'new states', and the real threat of a Mezzogiorno syndrome east of the Elbe. We have to consider psychology too. Many easterners blame westerners for profiting from reunification, for instance as a result of the actions of companies gaining access to fresh markets without making investment in production facilities.

Many westerners, on the other hand, complain that East Germans are simply not grateful for the largesse that has flowed across the former barbed wire of the old East–West border. These psychological problems of forging together East and West Germans at a time of much mutual resentment and recrimination have an economic dimension, and an economic cost.

Furthermore, we have to realise that many structural difficulties in the West German economy were diagnosed as serious weaknesses at the end of the 1980s. They include continuing large subsidies in areas like coal-mining, relative inflexibility in labour markets and the lack of a generalised capitalised pension system. In some sections of Germany's generally splendid manufacturing industry there has also been a reliance to rely on somewhat protected markets.

Many people, including Kohl and many leaders of banks and industry, made speeches in the late 1980s criticising the status quo and pleading for structural economic reforms to make the German economy properly prepared for the challenges of increasing European competition through the advent of the single market.[1] The drive for reform was however blunted by the overriding need to push through the adventure and the achievement of reunification. As is underlined by some of the problems facing Kohl's successor, Gerhard Schröder, in his first year in office, economic reform is still not a word that carries consensus. Furthermore, the obvious success and sheer wealth of the country – the solidity of the railway network, or the lavishness of luxury goods shops in the smallest of country towns – overlays and distracts attention from the deeper problems. The *Buddenbrooks* syndrome in Germany – taken from Thomas Mann's story of the well-to-do north German family caught in genteel decline – is alive and well:

> I know that the outward, visible and tangible signs and symbols of happiness and achievement often only appear when in reality everything is already starting to go downhill again. The outer signs take time to arrive – like the light of a star which shines most brightly when it is on the way to being extinguished, or maybe has already gone out.[2]

Yet there is another, more positive, side to the story too. The German corporate landscape is undergoing probably the furthest-reaching period of change since the Second World War. Judged by the rising trade surplus and by developments in unit wage costs in the last three years, Germany's industrial competitiveness has been improving rapidly,[3] thanks partly to a far better functioning of the pay bargaining system in the years after unification. Large German companies seem more likely than their counterparts in many other European countries to profit from Economic and Monetary Union (EMU), since in many cases they have the industrial and financial muscle to profit from the economies of scale possible across a larger single currency market.

There is far more industrial flexibility than commonly believed, emphasised by the way that BMW, the motor group, introduced flexible working practices into Rover, its UK subsidiary acquired in 1994. (These new practices were unfortunately not sufficient to stave off the sale of the subsidary by BMW in Spring 2000.) German industry has been embracing with gusto tenets of Anglo-American capitalism ranging from stock options to venture capital. The introduction of the euro, intensification of international competition and the obvious success in recent years of the US economic model have all created an environment for profound change in Germany. In many ways, the traditional Franco-German corporatist methods of economic governance – so-called 'Rhineland capitalism' – have been eroded in favour of a system leaning far more heavily towards Anglo-American *laissez-faire.*

The introduction of the single currency at the start of 1999 has on balance had a favourable impact on the German economy. Indeed, in a somewhat paradoxical way, Germany's economic problems, by lowering the gap between the higher- and lower-performing countries of Europe, have furthered the cause of convergence in continental Europe, and so aided the launch phase of the new currency. The euro's weakness has on the whole been welcome. The pick-up in German exports in 1999, and with it the improved performance of economic growth in the course of the year, has been directly attributable to the lower value of the new currency against the dollar, sterling and yen. From an internal point of view, the euro is strong, for the European inflation rate is very low. Externally, the euro has been weak – one could term it a sheep in wolf's clothing – but the reduction in the vulnerability of the German economy to variations of the exchange rate has been one of the positive side-effects desired by the architects of EMU. For all the possible long-term problems created by the largely unexpected external weakness of the euro, its first year of life has to be judged largely a success.

Is Germany in crisis?

One thing that will not happen is that the German system will undergo a real crisis. The German economic and political system is extremely resilient, partly as a result of post-war checks and balances placed to prevent the rise of anything akin to the extremism that so disastrously affected Germany, its neighbours and the rest of the world between 1933 and 1945. The checks and balances built into the federal political system may make decision-making often appear time-consuming and unwieldy, but this gives the country another form of defence mechanism against crisis. Like the Buddenbrook family, Germany has a great deal of built-in resistance. The outer signs of decline indeed take much time to arrive.

Everything from worker co-determination on the supervisory boards of large companies (introduced in the Ruhr coal and steel industry by the British occupying authorities in the early years after the war) to, now, the sharing of monetary responsibility with ten other countries through EMU are planks shoring up the great and soaring edifice of German economic solidity. As a result of these factors, Germany is never likely to undergo a period of highly evident, headline-grabbing cathartic change of the sort that has affected Britain and France since the 1980s. What we will see is a process of incremental, less evident change that in many ways can be equally significant. This will co-exist alongside many other more visible events that appear to indicate stagnation or – in the political field – even paralysis.

Even if more change is taking place than at first appears apparent, more will be necessary at the start of the next millennium. The tensions building up for reform in some notable areas of public policy such as pensions are now becoming very large. But full-scale catharsis will be avoided, and that is probably just as well. Germany's basic solidity is not in doubt, but there are legitimate questions whether the fundamental edifice of the country could cope without real trauma with the sort of changes that Thatcherism produced in the UK. The former president of the Bundesverband der Deutschen Industrie, Tyll Necker, once summed up Britain's greater capacity to submit to radical change: 'A seafaring people is better able to take knocks.' Of course, it is more complicated than that: precisely because Germany, in contrast to Britain's basic stability, has had so much fundamental *political* change since about the seventeenth century, it is more allergic than Britain to deep-rooted *economic* change.

German reunification was the greatest – and most unexpected of transitions, and in a sense the Germans have had more than enough change to worry about without coping with globalisation and European Union directives as well. Unification has been costly – German public debt, for instance, has grown from around DM 1 trillion to DM 2.3 trillion – but we must not forget that reunification on the West's terms during most of the period since 1945 would have been achieved at the expense of the Third World War. To that extent, the cost has been 'peanuts', to recall a phrase somewhat incautiously used by Hilmar Kopper, the former chief executive (now chairman of the supervisory board) of the Deutsche Bank commenting a few years ago on the losses caused by the bankrupt Schneider property group.

One impact of unification was the mismatch between German fiscal and monetary policy in the immediate years after the bringing together of the two German states. High Bundesbank interest rates in the early 1990s, directly a result of the adventurous fiscal policies put into effect by the father of unification, Helmut Keynes, were a proximate cause of Britain's departure from the exchange rate system of the European Monetary Union in 1992. This event still overshadows British politics and is an important reason dampening the enthusiasm even of pro-European Britons for joining EMU.

Schröder's first year

The first year of EMU coincided with the final phase in office of Helmut Kohl and the start of the new government of Gerhard Schröder. The Social Democrat-led government has made heavy weather of its first year, conspicuously failing to profit from the initial elan of the September 1998 election victory. Schröder made several grave mistakes. First, he gave his firebrand Finance Minister Oskar Lafontaine (who was also party chairman) far too much free rein in the aftermath of victory. Then Schröder did not succeed in stamping his own mark on policies by capitalising either on Lafontaine's tantrum-strewn departure or on his own subsequent election as SPD party chairman. The run of regional election defeats in autumn 1999 – although far from terminal for Schröder – and his party's collapse in the opinion polls brought a waning of the Chancellor's star. Almost as sudden was his recovery at the end of 1999 and the beginning of 2000 in the wake of the scandals over misuse of party financing affecting the Christian Democratic Union.

Schröder is a mix of contradictory personalities. As was apparent in the run-up to the September 1998 election, he is in many ways something of an old-fashioned Socialist and an interventionist. But he also has a better understanding of industry than Helmut Kohl. Schröder told me in 1998 that EMU would lead to more German companies taking over foreign ones – an ironic foretaste of his well-publicised antipathy to the hostile takeover bid for Mannesmann by the British–American Vodafone–Airtouch mobile telecommunications group.

Schröder has a firm opinion on which parts of the German system require reform. These include the pay-as-you-go pension system, where, as has been well documented since the 1980s, there is an urgent need for a transition to a supplementary scheme with an element of capitalisation, along the lines of schemes in several other European countries. But he has even more fixed ideas on areas of the system which can be left alone – such as pay bargaining, where he believes (probably justifiably) that plant-by-plant deals around the country have led to a much better adjustment between wages and costs than is indicated by the headline deals emerging from the country's elaborate centralised wage bargaining arrangements.

Schröder is no Tony Blair, no third way-ist, and he almost certainly now regrets bringing out with Blair the policy document on Social Democrat party modernisation that was issued at the beginning of June 1999. This was just before both the Labour Party and the SPD suffered heavy losses in the summer's European Parliament elections. Unlike Blair, Schröder is trying to prod his party gently towards modernisation while in government, and while fighting elections of one sort or another (as a result of Germany's federal system) almost every month. In addition, he has a far from enormous majority and has to rule with the unpredictable Greens.

Yet Schröder does have some important cards in his hand. If he does fall out with the Greens, he can form coalitions with either the liberal Free Democrats, or with the CDU (although this option, much canvassed at the last election, appears rather improbable at the moment). Rather like the Conservatives in the UK, the Christian Democrats will probably fail at the next election due in 2002.

Swings in German party politics tend to be long-term. Schröder, having suffered greatly from the SPD's lack of preparedness for government, will probably profit from economic pick-up in 2000–1 and a small demographically induced fall in unemployment in the next few years. He is likely to win the general election in 2002 and serve eight years as Chancellor – probably shaking off the Greens and, with luck, reforming the Social Democratic Party along the way. There is a strong possibility that the outcome that Schröder thought would happen in both 1994 and 1998

– a Grand Coalition with the Christian Democrats – will actually come about in 2002.

What future is there for German corporatism?

Charles de Gaulle spoke for many when he described Germany in a book published in 1934 as 'a bundle of powerful yet hazy instincts'.[4] There has been particular haziness since the end of the Second World War on the subject of the so-called economic miracle. One acquaintance of mine who used to work in TV recalls being dispatched at least half a dozen times to Germany since the 1980s years by his television producers to discover whether the much-acclaimed miracle was in fact well and truly over.

In recent times, it has been difficult to make up our minds on which of two equally inflated notions is actually true. To paraphrase Churchill, is the German economy at our feet or at our throats? It is very difficult to tell, since individual observers both within and outside Germany insist on drawing diametrically opposite sets of conclusions from the same basic sets of observations. The good news is equally balanced by the bad.

Take the newspapers, for instance. One set of articles tells us, 'Roll up the beach towels, the good life is over',[5] 'The evidence that Germany is slipping is unmistakable'[6] or 'Germany [is] Stalling'.[7] Read another set of clippings and you are told, on the other hand, 'Tomorrow belongs to Germany: Chancellor Kohl and his allies have managed to create through the ruthless exercise of political will the empire that Hitler failed to fashion in military conquest.'[8] or 'It's the good life for Germany's car workers – Longbridge workers facing sack and their overpaid, underworked Munich counterparts.'[9]

One set of observers would point to the high unemployment rate, the over-extended pensions system, the burgeoning subsidy bill for eastern Germany, the perceived inflexibility of the German labour markets, and the fact that German growth has lagged behind Britain's for much of the 1990s. In fact ever since the start of the 1970s German growth in most years apart from the boom times around unification (one has to say now, unhealthily overheated) has been below that of the average of industrial countries.

The closing weeks of 1999 brought a remarkable exposition of the strains on corporate Germany, not just as the result of the hostile bid for Mannesmann but also in the light of the near bankruptcy of the country's second largest building group, Philipp Holzmann. Even an authority as sober as Professor Otmar Issing, the former chief economist of the Bundesbank, now a member of the directorate of the European Central Bank, has termed Germany the new-found candidate to be 'the sick man of Europe.'

The latest forecasts from the OECD delivered in November 1999[10] sum up the state of affairs: after growth of only 1.3 per cent in 1999, Germany is expected to expand by 2.3 per cent in 2000 and 2.5 per cent in 2001. This is well below the growth rates expected for the European Union and the rest of the EMU area of 2.1 per cent in early 2000 and 2.8 per cent in the next two years. (The latest report from the German government's own Council of Economic Advisers is however slightly more optimistic on the growth front, forecasting that economic expansion in 2000 will pick up to 2.7 per cent after 1.4 per cent in 1999.)[11]

Another, much more confident, set of interpretations can also, however, be inferred. The Germans are not, after all, down to their last bratwurst, begging for pickings from the English holidaymakers speeding past on run-down Autobahnen on their way to Tyrolean holiday homes. Better-disposed commentators might point to the rising trade surplus, the low inflation rate or the sudden spurt during the late 1990s of smaller company flotations on the *Neuer Markt* section of the stock market. Deregulation in energy and telecommunications, initially slow to take off during the 1980s, has gathered pace in recent years, and has itself become a great impetus for corporate change in wide stretches of industry.

The rise in German unit wage costs, which was a key factor behind a sharp worsening of competitiveness in the early years after unification, has been reversed in the last few years as a result of a series of far more satisfactory wage rounds. According to the Institut der deutschen Wirtschaft, close to the BDI employers' organisation, unit labour costs per unit of output, although still among the highest in the world, are currently around 16 per cent below the level in the UK – a worrying sign of how British competitiveness has slipped under the impact of the high pound.[12]

Thanks, again, to a return to more orthodox economic policies in the last few years, the structure of German public spending has become somewhat more sound. Total state expenditure as a proportion of gross domestic product, at around 48 per cent, is in the middle ground of continental European performance (compared with 49 per cent in the Netherlands, 56 per cent in Denmark and 54 per cent in France). The British figure is 41 per cent. German banking, insurance, engineering, telecommunications, chemicals and motor groups have beefed up competitiveness, adopted new and more ruthless financing techniques, and have embarked on a series of take-over bids in which smaller rivals have been gobbled up. German investment in Britain – one of the most striking signs of German industrial intern[illegible]onalisation – has been a benefit for the British economy.

The merger of Dai[illegible] in which the Stuttgart-based company has [illegible]er), the take-over of Bankers Trust b[illegible] Bentley and Rolls–Royce by Volkswa[illegible] to tell a story of German corporate [illegible]

In most [illegible] themselves that public infrastructu[illegible]ore abundant and better quality th[illegible]. More important, but less visible, the ro[illegible] empire from central Europe has given the Gern[illegible] economic advantages against which the continued annu[illegible]nts to the east of 5 per cent western German GDP on roads, telecommunications, pensions and psychological support for 16 million East Germans appears the merest *bagatelle.*

The cliché that the Germans have been slow to embrace information technology is not borne out by the facts. Roughly 11 million Germans are now estimated to use the Internet – slightly more than in Britain – and the growth rate in coming years (25 million are forecast by 2003) is seen as higher than in any country in Europe. On-line stockbroking, for instance, is a far more attractive growth industry in Germany than in Britain.

Even though unemployment may be stuck around the 4 million level (and the true level of joblessness, taking into account those on early retirement and work support schemes in the east, is probably closer to 6 million) anecdotal evidence suggests that labour bottlenecks in high-tech parts of the economy are, if anything, greater than in Britain.

Perhaps the largest single indicator of Germany's corporate resilience is the strength of Germany's largest companies. The heavy-footed, long-lived joint stock corporations, in many cases still bearing their confident old nineteenth-century names, have been undergoing something of a revolution. The global trend of big German companies is in striking contrast to the relative provincialism of German politics.

The trials of Schröder's government have held back the growth in the German stock market in 1999, but the early months of 2000 saw a new wave of investor confidence. At the end of September 1999 the capitalisation of the French stock market exceeded that of Germany for the first time – an intriguing sign of just how much the French economy has been reformed in recent years. None the less, the wave of restructuring to make German companies more global, more cost-efficient, more open to shareholder interests and less reliant on their domestic production base adds up to the country's most drastic period of corporate reshaping since the Second World War.

Among the larger enterprises in Germany, the mergers between Veba and VIAG, on the one hand, and RWE and VEW on the other, in the utilities sector illustrate a trend towards greater concentration on companies' core businesses and away from earlier leanings towards conglomerates.

Mannesmann, which succumbed to a hostile bid from Vodafone in early 2000, has shown itself as an epitome of buccaneering capitalism as a result of its espousal of mobile phone technology during the 1990s. In the retail trade, we have seen sweeping changes at Metro and Karstadt. In chemicals, Hoechst has merged with the French group Rhône–Poulenc, with its headquarters in Strasbourg, to form a European leader in life sciences. Siemens has been transformed by the sale or spin-off of key parts of the business such as banking computer technology or semi-conductors that previous managements regarded as sacrosanct core components of the company's activities.

A huge question mark should, however, be placed against the performance of the large German banks. At home, they are struggling to cope with extreme competition and high costs in retail banking. One of the attempts to cope with these challenges, the merger between the two main Bavarian banks, Bayerische Hypobank and Bayerische Vereinsbank, has failed to deliver expected cost synergies and has led to an unseemly boardroom row and a spilling of much executive blood over unprofitable property loans in the east of the country.

On the international front, German banks have failed to shape up to the standards of American investment banking in their own European backyard. The main victors so far in the European market for financial services appear to have names like Merrill Lynch, Morgan Stanley and Goldman Sachs.

Concluding remarks

The result of Kohl's economic miscalculations is that, ten years after the fall of the Berlin Wall, Germany fulfilled neither the brightest hopes nor the direst apprehensions voiced in 1990. There are neither flourishing landscapes in east Germany, as Kohl predicted, nor significant signs of

Germany exerting its might on a European scale, as Mrs Thatcher feared.

As for European monetary union, it may help German corporate aggrandisement by giving a more secure outlet for much of German industry, but for the country as a whole, EMU exposes more weakness than strength.

The notion that Germany joined the euro at too high a rate, and that German industry is consequently languishing, is exaggerated. Trade statistics for 1998 and the first months of 1999 show that about half Germany's annual trade surplus of around $60 billion is recorded with countries that are part of EMU, and the proportion is growing. (Roughly one-fifth of the trade surplus is with Britain, a statistic that conveys the over-valuation of Britain's exchange rate but also underlines how grateful Germany should be to Britain for sucking in all these imports of cars, refrigerators and capital equipment.) On the other hand, the weakness of the euro clearly reflects some underlying problems not just of the euro area as a whole but also of its largest component, Germany. If the euro had not been formed, it would anyway have had to have been invented in 1999 through a much weaker performance of the D-Mark. (It is worth pointing out that, for much of the life of the old Federal Republic, the D-Mark was relatively weak in real terms, as the low West German inflation rate normally more than compensated for the rising nominal exchange rate.)

As Schröder predicted in 1998, large German corporations appear to be equipped to take advantage of the new single currency area than their counterparts in France, Italy or Spain. The contrast between successful German big business and growing social problems at home will continue to grow. There is a link here: these foreign take-overs have been accompanied by a continued shedding of jobs in Germany – hardly good news for the social fabric of Deutschland AG. Furthermore, the shareholders in Germany's new corporate behemoths are increasingly foreign fund management companies. The outcome of the Mannesmann battle (60 per cent owned by foreign firms) was decided far more in the banking parlours of London and New York than in the streets of the Ruhr.

It is worth reflecting for a moment on whether the fears of German domination openly expressed by Margaret Thatcher and her friends encouraged him in his naïve belief that the economic burdens of unification would be quickly overcome. If Germany really was as strong as the British were saying, so Kohl might well have thought, then it really would take only four years before the whole of the former German Democratic Republic was turned into a shiny new piece of up-to-date German capitalism.

Thatcher and Mitterrand (who if anything was even more worried about German dominance, but said so less loudly) may therefore have indirectly contributed to some of Kohl's grievously complacent mistakes over unification, notably his initial refusal to raise taxes and his over-generous treatment of East German workers and pensioners. Since these mistakes were the proximate causes of the Bundesbank decision to raise interest rates from summer 1991 onwards, the discomfort for the British and French economies caused by the German credit squeeze was partly self-imposed.

What will be the consequences of monetary union? The advent of the euro will speed up the internationalisation and the technological innovation of important parts of German industry. Large German companies have grown so contemptuous of the inadequate reform efforts of German politicians that they have had no choice but to embrace international expansion. However, many Germans, already suspicious about the new currency, may blame monetary union for the persistent high unemployment caused by the tendency of German companies to cut jobs at home in favour of foreign expansion.

Developments in Britain since the early 1980s – successful deregulation and innovation in important parts of the economy, accompanied by a growing wealth and income gap between the 'haves' and 'have-nots' – provide a foretaste of possible German experience in coming years. As two countries which have often appeared to represent different poles of economic success and failure, Germany and Britain will continue to remain mirror images of each other in many areas. As one example of this, Britain is likely to remain outside EMU until 2004 at least – and will suffer no great drawbacks as a result of its self-exclusion from the euro area. Mutually beneficial competition between different systems of economic governance in the UK and Germany is due to remain one of the enlivening features of the European economy for well into the twenty-first century.

Notes

1 See for instance, Wilfried Guth, then chairman of the supervisory board of the Deutsche Bank, 'The German engine has lost steam quite considerably. The virtues which characterised the first post-war period – courage to liberalize and accept full competition, a firm belief in the free market model – are still accepted as basic principles, but often neglected in practice.' (Frankfurt, 2 October 1987) or Tyll Necker, then president of the Bundesverband der

Deutschen Industrie, 'We are thinking too much about our prosperity and not enough about our future' (Cologne, 13 October 1987).

2 Thomas Mann, *Buddenbrooks.*

3 According to the Institut der deutschen Wirtschaft, unit wage costs fell more than 3 per cent between 1996 and 1998, reducing the traditional gap between Germany's costs and those of most of its industrial trading partners.

4 Charles de Gaulle, *Vers l'armée de métier.*

5 *Daily Mail,* 26 February 1996.

6 *Sunday Times,* 18 October 1998.

7 *Evening Standard,* 18 March 1999.

8 *Sunday Times,* 28 March 1998.

9 *The Express,* October 25 1998.

10 OECD Economic Outlook, 16 November 1999.

11 Sachverständigenrat, Jahresgutachten 1999/2000, 16 November 1999.

12 Informationsdienst des Instituts der deutschen Wirtschaft, 28 October 1999.

6

The end of the innovation economy?

Rebecca Harding and David Soskice[1]

Introduction

The German system of innovation in general and its system of technology transfer in particular has long been admired for producing a supportive environment within which companies can innovate (Freeman 1995; Fitzroy *et al.* 1998; Vitols 1997; Carlin and Soskice 1997; Soskice 1996). Whilst historically this system has not produced the radical, path-breaking innovations found, for example, in America, it is a model to which academics, politicians and business people alike have long looked for inspiration in directing policy in their own countries. Two key factors give the model such appeal:

1 *The capacity of the German economy consistently to produce high quality, high technology and highly competitive products.* This is particularly true in five industries: chemicals, pharmaceuticals, mechanical engineering, automobiles and electronics (Cantwell and Harding 1998); and
2 The strength of the German economy in incremental innovations on the basis of established technologies, again in the technological areas listed above (Soskice 1994).

In recent years, however, it appears that policy debates, both academic and practical, have increasingly drawn upon the American model for their inspiration (*The Economist*, w/b 7 Nov. 1998). There are two principal reasons for this. First, the German model has recently appeared to be floundering. R&D expenditure fell by 0.6 per cent of GDP between 1989 and 1996. Although this was part of a world-wide trend in reduction of R&D as a percentage of GDP, there have been simultaneous, and perhaps more worrying trends in German technology which have concerned commentators. In particular, the share of hi-tech goods in German exports fell during the early 1990s and the German economy looked as though it was becoming a net importer of technology intensive products (*Spiegel* 35/1998). The German innovation system appeared incapable of responding to this challenge. It was argued that the very nature of the system was reflective: it could only transfer technology to users at their request meaning that any prototype development was an incremental innovation on the basis of existing technology rather than a radical breakthrough. As such, it was argued, the 'system' was relatively weak in supporting German companies in fast-growing areas like IT.

The second reason for the German model's reduced appeal is the ascendency of the new 'global-market paradigm' which began to emerge during the 1990s, based on the Anglo-Saxon approach to markets generally and innovation in particular. The combination of a *laissez-faire* approach to competition for public research funding and a venture capital market which provides substantial incentives to entrepreneurs has an obvious appeal to policy-makers wanting to stimulate competitive advantage through radical innovation. A complex, quasi-coordinated system like the German appears unresponsive and inflexible in comparison.

The purpose of this chapter is to argue that despite such criticisms, there are still powerful reasons for believing in the strength of the German innovation system. It argues that the coordinated and systematic appearance of the system hides an inherent, competitive, market-based dynamic at a micro level. The innovation market in Germany is highly contested: there is competition between and within technology transfer institutes for public and private money. Thus there exists within the system both market based incentives and, critically, strong public support for innovation which reflects the public nature of research in itself and its private exploitation. This combines with the 'collaborative' approach for which the German system is renowned and with a new focus at a policy level on hi-tech areas to create a system which is both strong and, critically, well-resourced, despite the net decline in R&D expenditure reported above.

The nature of the German research and technology system

The post-war technology transfer system was a by-product of both Allied attempts to divide up research expertise and divorce it from direct sources of government control, and the legacy of existing structures (Hohn and Schimank 1990). For example, the Max Planck Society, was founded in 1948 from the Kaiser-Wilhelm Society (first founded in 1911 and funded by companies). After the war, Max Planck Institutes received funding from individual states (*Länder*) to conduct independent, basic research in areas to complement the broad research remit of Higher Education Institutes (HEIs). By 1964, the *Länder* pooled resources for basic scientific research to form the 'global' funding with the Bund (federal government) that now exists. Two points are important here: first, that the basic research conducted by Max Planck Institutes is independent of either central government or corporate funding, and second, that it does not have a broad research remit. Thus, while HEIs for example are obliged to conduct research in every area, Max Planck Institutes can select priorities and specialise their focus in accordance with perceived scientific need.

There is, then, a 'linear cascade' structure that exists in the German technology transfer system (Hohn and Schimanck 1990; Hohn 1998; RH interviews 1998). The structure originated to ensure three things: independent basic scientific research (through the Max Planck Institutes), large-scale structures for 'big science' of national or strategic importance, and transferability through intermediate applied research institutes to the end industrial users. This is illustrated in figure 6.1 below.

Basic research is conducted largely by the institutes of the Max Planck

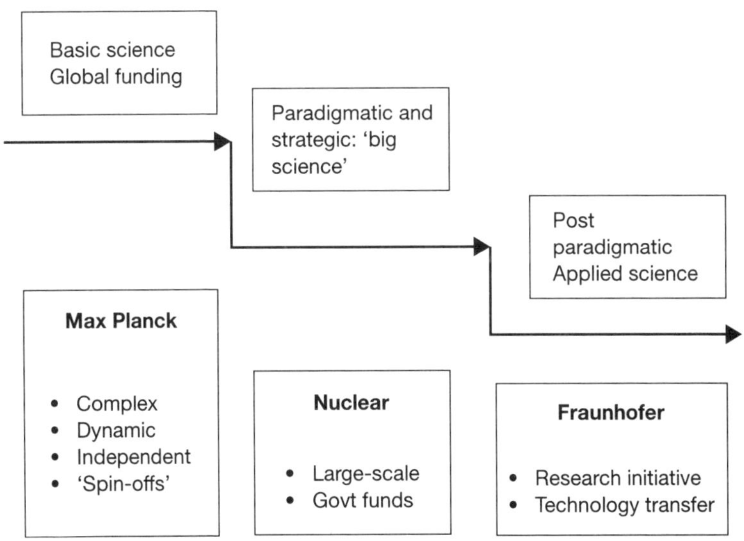

Source: Hohn 1998 RH Interviews July 1998.

Figure 6.1 **The cascade model of technology transfer**

Society and by HEIs. Core funding at this basic level is from the *Länder* (either individually or from the 1964 agreement) and from public contracts. 'Paradigmatic' or strategic research is conducted by large laboratories, government research institutes and 'Blue List' task-oriented and large-scale research institutes. The Blue List institutes are funded on a 50–50 basis by the Bund and the *Länder*. Applied ('post-paradigmatic') research is conducted by technology transfer institutes, most notably the Fraunhofer, and funded jointly by Bund, and Industrial sources on a contract basis (the *Länder* contribution is small).

The R&D system: details of funding and structure

But figure 6.1 hides the complexity of government funding for technology transfer. The actual organisation of the German R&D system is illustrated in figure 6.2 below.

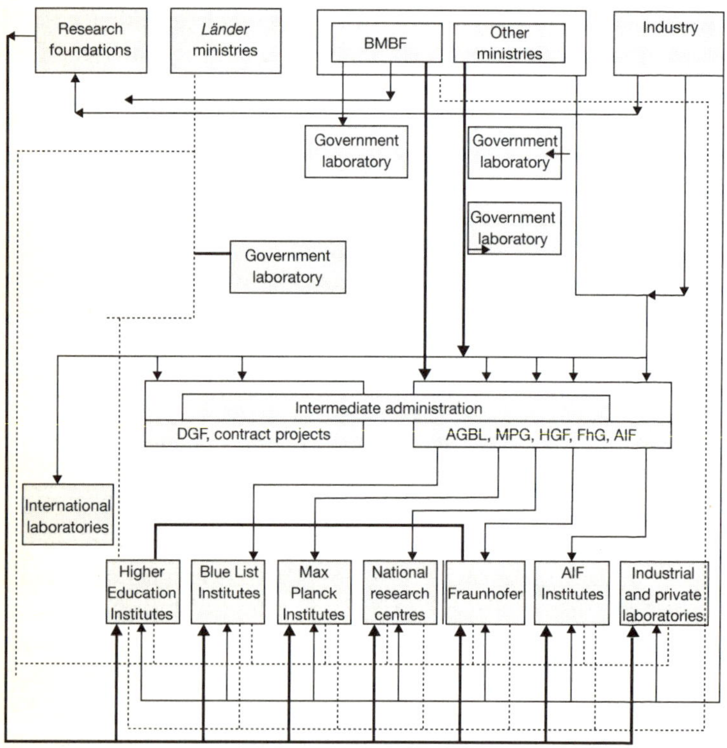

Source: Simplified from Krull and Meyer-Kramer 1999.

Figure 6.2 **Organisation of the German R&D system**

To argue that the system is complex is something of an understatement as is clearly illustrated by figure 6.2. Above this structure are the *Länder* and the federal government (Bund), the National Science Council and the Conference of Ministers for Cultural Affairs, Education, Arts and Science. These supervisory bodies set funding targets and priorities. Figure 6.2 highlights several interesting points:

1 *The multiplicity of funding sources for each of the independent technology transfer institutions* (Universities, Fraunhofer, Max Planck etc). These institutes receive monies from a total of four sources: industry, research foundations, *Länder* and the BMBF (and other federal ministries).
2 *The inter-relatedness of funding.* In their turn, both the ministries and industry provide funds to the research foundations.
3 *The rigid and hierarchical funding structure.* Funding from governmental sources goes towards R&D and towards the administration of R&D: the intermediate administrations of the Fraunhofer (FhG), the Max Planck Institutes (MPG), the Blue List Institutes (AGBL), the National Research Centres (e.g. Hermann von Helmholtz Gesellschaften) and Industrial Research Institutions (AiF) all accrue monies from the *Länder*, the Federal government and from industry separately, although some of this is passed on to specific research scientists and projects.
4 *The relative independence of government laboratories.* In a structure which so greatly facilitates technology transfer, it is, perhaps, remarkable that the funding of government laboratories is simply from government sources.
5 *Each of these separate intermediate organisations has responsibility for research in clearly delineated areas.* A tacit 'research cartel' exists between the largest R&D structures within the technology transfer system (RH interviews, July 1998). For example, the FhG Specializes in strategic and applied research for government and industry with a focus on the development of new technologies in microelectronics, civil and mechanical engineering, materials, environmental research and innovation studies. Until recently it has had little presence in biotechnology as it leaves this area of research to the Max Planck Institutes who have core competences in basic research in related areas, largely in diagnostics. However, as a result of twentieth-century German history, there is a public (and constitutional) resistance, particularly to genetic research within Germany. Thus biotechnological and genetic research tended to be conducted by small companies abroad

(especially the USA). These companies operate independently but are owned by German private sector large companies such as Hoechst, Bayer and Siemens.

The Max Planck Institutes also have a presence in humanities research, as do the Blue List Institutes. The Blue List Institutes conduct specific scientific research projects while the Hermann von Helmholtz institutes conduct research across a whole spectrum of areas from basic science to mission-driven research. Germany's 89 universities and, increasingly, the 180 Fachhochschulen play a central role in the transfer of technology between the teaching and the research function (see also Schmoch 1998). The Fachhochschulen tend to complement research conducted in universities through their focus on applied technologies. Universities and Fachhochschulen are increasingly competitive for shares of the state and federal research budgets with the intermediate research institutes. The overheads of these Higher Education Institutes (HEIs) are met through federal and teaching budgets. Their costs are considerably lower than those say, of a FhG. Further, the BMBF recognises the importance of patenting activity from Higher Education sources and has funded research looking at ways of improving this source of innovative activity (Becher *et al.* 1996).

Despite the complexity of the technology transfer and funding structure however, funding priorities are clearly defined according to the targets set at a federal level. These priorities are set irrespective of the nature or source of funding. Some targets are not set according to priorities but are focused on particular R&D performers (for example the FhG) who have autonomy in the allocation of funds to priority areas identified by demand.

German R&D remains concentrated in traditional manufacturing industries: automobiles, electrical and non-electrical machinery, electronic and communication equipment and industrial chemicals (Abramson *et al.* 1997). The result is patenting activity that is clearly focused in these areas of traditional economic strength (Cantwell and Harding 1998). For constitutional reasons, there has been very little R&D in defence related areas and aerospace (just 8 per cent and 6 per cent of the total budget respectively), as indicated above. German companies were, until recently, reluctant to undertake biotechnology research in general and genetic research in particular for societal and administrative reasons. This is reflected in the large number of companies which own overseas companies who conduct this research for them (this is particularly noticeable in the German ownership of small US biotechnology companies) (Cantwell and Harding 1998).

Evaluation of the system

Critics of the German system argue that it is top-heavy, complex and unresponsive. The cascade system illustrated in figure 6.1 might appear organised and highly successful in some areas (such as, for example, nuclear technology and environmental research), but it has noticeably failed to succeed in leading-edge technologies like IT (Hohn 1998; Mason and Wagner 1999). The cascade structure was developed to separate the private and public sector beneficiaries of scientific research. In areas such as nuclear and environmental research the distinction between 'public goods' and private profit are relatively easily made and this is reflected in the sources of funding for such research within Germany. In IT, where technological change is rapid and private returns to innovation very high, the beneficiaries of research are less clearly delineated. Thus a technology transfer system based on an assumption that there is a clear delineation between the two that can be reflected in funding is bound to be relatively weak in radical innovation.

Criticisms such as this have resulted in the changes to the funding structure which are now beginning to emerge. Universities are gaining increasing proportions of their research funding from industry (rising from 4 per cent to 8 per cent of total funding for basic scientific research and up to 20 per cent of the total funding for applied research). They are increasingly competitive with, for example, the FhG for industry funded contract research. A FhG scientist costs approximately DM 22,000 per month per project (including insurances, travel and subsistence, overheads and salary costs). Indeed, some estimates of FhG costs by interviewees at high-cost institutes were as high as DM 35,000 per month. In contrast, a university scientist will cost around DM 12,000 per month, as the university pays overheads. As the qualifications of the two scientists are the same, public-sector organizations in particular increasingly contract research from the universities (RH interviews April 1998). The AN-institutes (contract research establishments affiliated to but independent of universities and Fachhochschulen and with a particular focus on biotechnology and IT research) are a product of this new competitive environment but, as they must pay their overheads, their costs are roughly equivalent to the cheaper Fraunhofer Institutes (*Technologie Nachrichten* 1998).

However, it would be unwise to discount the cascade system as irrelevant in a world characterised by radical innovations. Incremental product innovation will always be important as radical scientific research develops into marketable products. The German economy has historically proven itself resilient to major shifts in techno-economic paradigms and, on the basis of research conducted for this chapter, there is no reason to suggest that the latest phases of IT or biotechnology should be any different. There are numerous reasons for this.

First, institutions have existed within the German technology transfer system that reflect the market-based incentive structures that support radical innovation. For example, AN-institutes emerged in the late 1990s as major sources of dynamism and comparative advantage in innovation. These structures are not new, however. AN-institutes were first established in the mid-1970s to plug the perceived hole in the cascade model that meant that prototypes were not reaching the market as viable products. The AN-institutes, funded largely by contract research, were given clear incentives to assist in the production of such marketable goods. The contract research funding of AN-institutes, and even of Fraunhofer, is still not risk capital in that the research institutes are non-profit organisations. However, as will be seen below, this does not preclude the dynamic of profit-type incentives since many of the AN-institutes have subsidiary limited liability companies affiliated to them.

Second, large companies further exhibit this 'externalisation of risk' at a corporate level by technological 'outsourcing'. The example of biotechnology has been given above. Partnerships with small venture capital companies, frequently but not exclusively based abroad, allow large companies to concentrate on core businesses but simultaneously to develop new technologies. The domestic biotechnology market is accordingly strengthening (Casper 1998)

Third, while large companies conduct, say, biotechnology research through small venture capital companies, technology transfer institutes like Fraunhofer and AN-institutes conduct research and develop prototypes in equipment manufacture which will allow them to compete even in the newly emerging technological markets. Thus, for example, medical instrumentation and diagnostic equipment are expanding areas of research in Max Planck, Fraunhofer and AN-institutes.

Fourth, a system of pre-competitive research 'sharing' exists through the Industrial Research Associations (AiF). These are groups of SMEs who, unable to fund applied research themselves, join together jointly to participate in pre-competitive research leading to prototype development. Although much of this collaborative research is arguably *competi-*

tive (RH interviews 1998), the AiF are an increasingly important structure within the system since they provide networks which span the technology transfer system, and provide access to innovation and hi-tech markets which would otherwise be out of reach for many small companies. The AiF structure is argued to counter-balance the large company financial bias of Fraunhofer and Max Planck Institutes[2] (Hohn 1999; RH interviews 1998).

Fifth, further 'networking' systems at a regional level exist through the Steinbeis Foundations, first established in 1971. These are applied research and consultancy units, which exist within HEIs, particularly Fachhochschulen. The major concentration of individual Steinbeis Technology Transfer Centres is within Baden-Württemberg but the Steinbeis Foundation's networks extend across Germany and abroad, especially in Europe. A technology transfer centre is usually led by a Fachhochschule Professor and staffed largely by students (usually writing final year or post-graduate dissertations). The projects are small and the companies using the Steinbeis service are usually from a 20–30km radius of the centre. But, although the role of Steinbeis is heavily debated, they undeniably fulfil an important role in networking and knowledge sharing (RH interviews July 1998).

Sixth, policy is changing to encourage overseas and domestic R&D back into Germany, while increasing emphasis is being placed on the area of biotechnology research. These were published as guidelines by the BMBF in July 1996. The whole funding structure of the German R&D system in general and technology transfer in particular is becoming more competitive with traditional 'quasi-monopolies' of public funds, such as the FhG, increasingly competitive with a range of higher education and dedicated research institutes for funding.

Finally, any suggestion that the thrust of Fraunhofer work is supportive rather than developmental hides the capacity of the Fraunhofer to re-invent itself. Each Fraunhofer institute has a different character and a unique 'tacit knowledge' pool. Faced with the competitive threat of the equally qualified but cheaper AN-institutes, cooperative structures have developed between and within Fraunhofer Institutes which are evolving to avoid duplication, and hence to reduce overheads but which also integrate the combined strengths of the whole system. Thus, FhG/TEG, was established in 1982 with the idea of creating synergies between individual Fraunhofer Institutes in an holistic approach to industrial contracts. Its 'technology transfer' includes the codified knowledge of scientists in product development and the tacit knowledge of systems and management consultants to support process development. The role of TEG and other Fraunhofer is discussed substantially below. Suffice to say here that TEG has been enormously successful and has grown substantially throughout the 1990s (Hohn, 1998, 1999).

Changing customer specifications and the perceived importance of radical innovation render the system prone to criticism in the face of the globalization of economic activity and rapidly advancing technology. But within the system appears to be a tacit capacity to *adapt* to change. Thus, the system is proving remarkably resilient to major structural change while adapting incrementally to the external forces which require it to change. The Fraunhofer, for example, has structural advantages in its size and the focus on technology foresight which pervades individual institutes[3]. Further, funding in Germany is still for 'scientific excellence' and remains substantial. The 'emergent', although not new, technology transfer structures serve the interests of Mittelstand companies perhaps better through their networks, cooperation and competition with one another. These are also the structures that favour radical innovation. And in no sector of the technology transfer system examined in the context of this paper was there evidence of shortage of funds[4] – indeed, since Fraunhofer and AN-institutes are non-profit making organisations, some representatives complained of having 'too much money' (RH interviews 1998)!

The role of the Fraunhofer Society

Funding and structure

It is the Fraunhofer Society which is the popular image of the transfer mechanism between basic science and product and process application in Germany. Within the context of the whole R&D system illustrated in figure 6.2 above, the Fraunhofer may seem a relatively small part. But with 8,900 employees (of which almost one half are scientists and engineers.), a total budget of DM 1.3 billion in 1996 and over 25 years in applied R&D and technology transfer, the organisation can neither be described as insignificant nor easily undermined. During 1995/96 it grew by 200 employees, increased its total contract research by 9 per cent and increased total non-government funding by 16 per cent. The overall increase in core funding allocated to research was 3 per cent, a figure which compensates for the heavy loss of public project funding which fell to less than 16 per cent during 1995/6.

The Fraunhofer Gesellschaft zur Förderung der angewandeten Forschung (FhG) is a network of some 48 separate institutes of which there are some 36 in the old states of Germany and 12 in the new, East German states. Further, the FhG is establishing itself as a major intermediate technology transfer institution abroad. For example, in the United States, Brazil and China the FhG presence is particularly strong and supportive of both indigenous industry and of German companies operating overseas. Developing activities in the UK and the Netherlands are adding to the FhG's international portfolio.

Funding comes largely from government and industry in one-third ratios: the *Drittellösung*, as illustrated in figure 6.3. This means that one-third is core funding (from Fraunhofer headquarters, but originating from government sources), one-third is public contract research and the remaining third is funding from industrial research contracts. Ninety per cent of the core funding from government comes from the federal level and the remainder from the Land in which a particular institute is based.

Although the ratio of contract to core funding is 2:1, the actual quantity of money that a Fraunhofer Institute receives annually will depend on

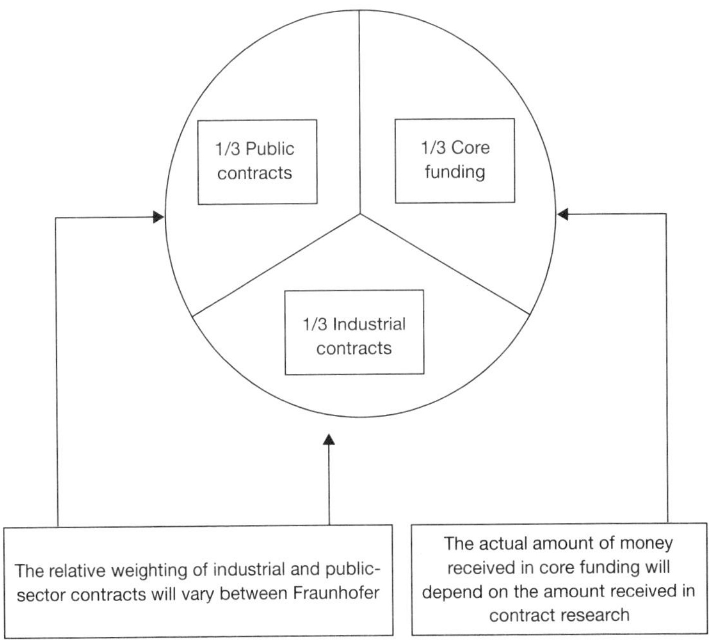

Figure 6.3 **The funding structure of the Fraunhofer Institutes**

the amounts received in contract research. This 'pound for pound' funding rewards entrepreneurial behaviour and goes some way to explaining the sustained growth of the Fraunhofer Society. Each Deutschmark gained from a contract is matched and multiplied in a variable ratio by core funding as illustrated in figure 6.4.

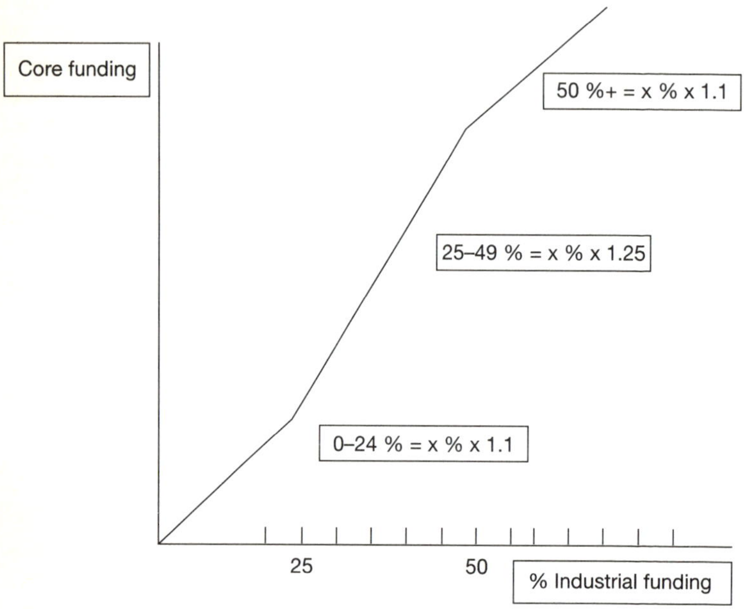

Figure 6.4 **Incremental increases in core funding relative to industrial funding**

The calculation process is complex. Each Fraunhofer institute raises non-core funding (i.e. two-thirds) from either public research or industrial research contracts. However, the exact balance of public and industrial research varies between Fraunhofer. An institute which has less than 25 per cent of total turnover accounted for by industrial contracts will receive proportionately less than an institute which has, like TEG for example, nearly 80 per cent of its turnover sourced from industrial contracts. Matched core funding up to 25 per cent of total funding is met by an incremental ratio of 0.1 per cent; over 25 per cent is in a ratio of 0.25 per cent. Thus, TEG receives the first 25 per cent in a ratio of 0.1 per cent, 26–50 per cent in a ratio of 0.25 per cent and the remainder in a ratio of

0.1 per cent. All calculations are made retrospectively, i.e. based on turnover figures for the preceding year. Thus no Fraunhofer can be certain of how much money it will receive in a given year until 31 December of the previous year.

FhG institutes are established on the basis of perceived demand for contracted project research. An institute can be established if it can demonstrate that it will be able to achieve the required two-thirds of contract funding through project work over the next three years. So, for example there are just 7 institutes which focus on microelectronics research in Germany because demand is small while demand in mechanical engineering is relatively high in Germany (reflecting the technological strengths of its indigenous industry) and, hence accounts for a larger number of institutes. Environmental technologies are strong in the FhG portfolio but biotechnology is relatively weak. Of its 48 institutes, all bar 6 have civilian R&D as their focus.

The Fraunhofer are particularly, although not exclusively, strong in supporting the needs of SMEs. They act as catalysts for technology transfer between basic science and industry by providing scientists who work on the development of product prototypes based on new innovations in laboratories and higher education establishments. This is effected through the close contacts that FhG scientists have with research scientists in universities.

It is further aided by the contacts that the FhG have beyond the immediate technology transfer system into the wider innovation and corporate governance systems referred to above. For example, the Deutsche Bank has long acknowledged the structural weakness of the German financial system in encouraging venture capital projects, particularly from SME's. Thus, it now pays the FhG a consultancy fee (estimated at around DM 20000 per project) for its scientists to evaluate venture capital-type proposals (RH interviews April, July 1998; Kluth and Andersen 1997).

The role of Fraunhofer Institutes

Expectations of the FhG are high: that its institutes will, 'contribute to the innovative strength of the German economy' by identifying innovative potential, meeting demand of industry and adapting existing technologies to meet public and private sector needs (Krull and Meyer-Kramer 1997). A FhG scientist has a unique role as both a researcher and a scientific consultant – the onus is on the individual scientist to make the transfer system effective. In principle, the scientist will not advise per se but will work on applied research with a practitioner (say from the end user) with the objective of balancing practical need with scientific feasibility. Consultants are employed separately to establish market need and design and develop products beyond a prototype stage.

This facilitating role, combined with the scientific and practical expertise of FhG researchers means that, despite increased competition, the FhG has comparative advantage in effective technology transfer between basic science and research which is further enhanced by Foresight programmes and its patenting evaluation activities and networks with external experts (RH interviews April, July 1998). Thus, although the subject expertise of a university and a FhG scientist may be identical, the latter has cumulative competence in the technology transfer relationship between the science base and the end practitioner. This cumulative expertise is strongest in the traditional areas of focus within the German economy and the role of the FhG scientists is arguably to reinforce traditional areas of strength rather than to develop new ones (RH interviews April 1998).

Increasingly, however, universities, and particularly the Technische Fachhochschulen are gaining strength (and funding) both in the traditional areas of technology transfer and in new areas such as biotechnology. The relationship between consultants and scientists on a technology transfer project is not always clearly delineated and companies are beginning to require product development as part of the research contract. The FhG is losing its monopoly of government funding.

'But,' argued one interviewee, 'you can't just get rid of 25 years of expertise.' With a dynamism that would answer the sternest critic, the FhG is changing to incorporate the dynamism of markets and the cumulative expertise of collaboration. For example, its newest institutes, such as the Technologie-Entwicklungsgruppe (TEG) in Stuttgart do focus on product development and are more market-based in their outlook while the Institute for Systems and Innovation Research (ISI) has increasing presence in biotechnology research through partnerships with other Fraunhofer Institutes and its own biotechnology department. It does have an increasing presence in biotechnology research and, like its corporate counterparts, is increasingly internationalising its activities in order both to support German companies abroad and to provide a model of technology-transfer to overseas companies in their own environment.

Individual Fraunhofer Institutes: a case study of symbiotic tension

Each Fraunhofer Institute has its own characteristics and its own expertise and only through an examination of the activities of individual institutes can a true picture of the nature of German technology transfer through the Fraunhofer be developed (see Harding 1999b). Interestingly, although research activity is carefully delineated at a systemic level, as shown in the cascade model, at the level of technology transfer there is no such delineation nor even a division of labour between separate institutes to avoid duplication (RH interviews July 1998). Indeed, duplication exists both between and within institutes. Sometimes this leads to collaboration and at other times to competition. The result is a *symbiotic tension*, where each institute and each department within each institute is dependent on the others continuing in research excellence for both the evolution of know-how *and* the dynamism of market-based competition.

Individual Fraunhofer researchers and scientists are profoundly aware of the criticisms levelled at the Fraunhofer Society as a whole. In particular they point out that the Fraunhofer model does not provide an effective means for generating radical technologies. Research is conducted at the request of companies or public bodies and Fraunhofer Institutes individually cannot compete with the huge laboratories of companies like Siemens employing some 8,000 people in R&D.

But, the critical issue for any Fraunhofer is how to make a particular technology implementable. This is incremental innovation and rests on three factors: awareness of technological developments in the future, ideas of how to implement this technology cost-effectively and innovatively and, accordingly, knowledge of customer requirements. Increasingly, customer specifications are changing: they require less in the way of technology transfer (scientific or codified know-how) and more in the way of *knowledge* transfer (technical, or tacit, know-how). There is thus a blurring of the distinction between the role of 'scientist' and 'consultant'. While the scientific and applied research role of Fraunhofer researchers is no less important under this structure, there is a market-based need to combine this cumulative scientific experience with *knowledge* of how a particular innovation will work once implemented.

Each Fraunhofer Institute has a unique combination of this codified and tacit know-how although the *actual* scientific base of particular institutes may be similar. Thus, for example, the Technology Development Group (TEG), the Institute for Production and Automation (IPA) and the Institute for Production and Design (IPK) have similar, and competitive, core competencies. Each stresses the importance of collaboration and networking in their research. However, their cumulative *knowledge* which is transferred to customers in specific projects is different and may be simultaneously complementary and conflicting. This is the essence of the *symbiotic tension* which is the strength of the technology transfer system generally and of the Fraunhofer in particular.

Collaborative competition

A case study illustrates the potential that this symbiotic tension lends the Fraunhofer system in adapting its system of technology transfer to new paradigms. While it may seem unwise to rely on one case study, the findings and interpretations of this case were corroborated, both through the survey of experts and through other case studies during the research period (see also Harding 1999b). The example here, however, is particularly suitable as it illustrates the unique potential for collaboration and competition within the Fraunhofer.

Fraunhofer ISI (FhG/ISI) was working with a large engineering company with a substantial industrial product portfolio to develop new, competitive application products within a ten-year time scale and with the potential to add to world-wide turnover by some DM 30 million. The project was in its second phase. The first phase had focused on establishing the needs of the client and their customers through a series of interviews, a workshop and use of technology foresight (Delphi) data on the electronics industry based on existing research at ISI. This first phase had produced some 21 product ideas, ranging from incremental adaptations of existing capacity to radical innovations involving high risk, but with potentially greater market return.

The second phase, another workshop, was intended to be a forum for discussing each of these ideas, and any others that emerged from a brainstorming session. The ultimate goal was to narrow the number of ideas down to a manageable quantity such that business plans for each could be constructed in the final phase. But a second purpose of the workshop was to create networks and partnerships between the client and other Fraunhofer Institutes. Accordingly, representatives from four Fraunhofer Institutes, ISI, TEG, IPK and IPA were all present, as was an academic from the University of Karlsruhe, who also had affiliations to the applied university–industry research institute there, the Centre for Research in IT (FZI).

It is not the purpose here to evaluate the way in which the workshop was operated or to assess its eventual outcome. What is interesting in the context of this chapter, is the appearance of four, normally competitive, institutes focusing their discussion on one issue. The rivalry between TEG, IPA and IPK was highly developed: TEG as an institute evolved from IPA structures and all three competed aggressively for similar client projects. Thus, while the three normally came into contact through 'market-based' activities, they were here cooperating as experts in a product development project.

This cooperation approach was more familiar to TEG than to the other Fraunhofer Institutes. TEG has a core competence in mechanical and electrical engineering, including its own workshop and design function. When it is approached by customers to conduct a project, it will buy in expertise from elsewhere if it does not have appropriate in-house capacity, for example from other Fraunhofer, from universities and from industrial groups. TEG's presentation was accordingly informal and integrative and very much focused on client needs. Despite the fact that TEG and IPA had collaborated on other product development research (including Lufthansa's 'Skywash' sensor-based aeroplane cleaner), the other two institutes were, perhaps, less familiar with the 'knowledge sharing' format of the occasion. Both gave formal presentations about themselves and their own research and 'expert' capabilities which were interesting in their own right, but rather less focused on client needs.

The 'hidden agenda' of the day was to create an ideal collaborative partnership between participants which would lead to profitable product development in the third and final stage. Thus IPA was to provide expertise on electrical and mechanical engineering, TEG was to provide similar expertise effectively combined with their 'whole systems' approach to engineering problems, while IPK provided input in microelectronics and design. ISI was to retain its coordinating role and had a clear view of the strengths of each Institute that could be brought to the project[5].

Concluding remarks

There are two problems faced by any company seeking to innovate. The first is the need of companies to translate scientific advances into a form suitable for the company's own process or product technology. The second is the difficulty of incorporating radical innovations in newly emerging technologies. In addressing both of these problems, the German system generally and technology policy in particular appears remarkably suitable for sustaining the country's traditional strengths in producing hi-tech and high value-added incremental innovations and adapting itself, albeit relatively slowly, to exogenous paradigm shifts. The inherent dynamism of the system is such that it can successfully incorporate both markets *and* new innovations. What is remarkable about the German system is its capacity to anticipate and pre-empt changes and to adapt appropriately when the need arises. We see no reason to doubt that this trend will continue.

Notes

1 This chapter is derived from work conducted by Rebecca Harding, published as chapter 6 in Lissenburgh and Harding (2000) and from Soskice (1994, 1996).

2 More than 40 per cent of Fraunhofer contracts come from companies with less than 500 employees. It is nevertheless true to state that the *financial* contribution of larger companies is greater.

3 For example, the Delphi project at Fraunhofer ISI and the 'expert survey' at Fraunhofer TEG. Other 'foresight' functions are apparent in other Institutes too (for example, FhG Institute for Biomedicine).

4 The resourcing of individual institutes depends to a large extent on the nature of demand for their research activities. Thus TEG, IPK and IPA are all highly successful organisations with a close market orientation. Other institutes, for example in microelectronic or environmental technologies, are less well resourced.

5 The final stage of the project was being developed during the latter part of 1998. At the time of writing it appeared that TEG would be developing two of the products with the company and IPA the third. ISI would retain its coordinating and facilitating role.

7
German corporatism: dead or alive?

Rebecca Harding and Arndt Sorge

Introduction

High unemployment, persistent net capital outflows from Germany, high labour costs and, most recently, the takeover of Mannesmann by Vodafone–Airtouch have lent renewed energy to the 'German corporatism is dead' school of commentary (*Guardian*, 29 Jan. 2000). German firms are constrained by the rigidities of the *Mitbestimmung* (or co-determination) law which allows for equal representation at a supervisory level in the largest German companies. There has been evidence through the decades that this tends to favour the interests of capital rather than labour (Kittner 1982; Harding 1995; Lane 1989; Maurice *et al.* 1986), thus the structures of union representation themselves cannot be 'blamed' for inflexibility. But co-determination is itself part of a complex triangle of corporation law including the *Betriebsverfassungsgesetz* (Works Constitution Act) and the Aktiengesetz (Shareholdings Act) which form the base of *Modell Deutschland.* Thus equal representation combines with a complex shareholder proxy voting system and a relatively weak equity market, to favour long-termism and incremental change rather than dynamic change.

The result is a persistent picture of the largest German companies as hierarchical and bureaucratic – lumbering, slow and unresponsive to changes in the market. A recent article in *Wirtschaftswoche* pointed out that German companies are substantially smaller in terms of market capitalisation than their counterparts elsewhere in the world. This is illustrated in table 7.1 which gives the market capitalisation of the German companies in the top 100 companies across ten key sectors (measured in billions of euros).

Table 7.1 shows that German companies are, indeed, small in terms of market capitalisation relative to the largest players in the sectors shown here. Daimler–Chrysler, for example is the second largest company in the world but is still only some 39 per cent of the size of Toyota. Similarly, the Deutsche Bank is double the size of its nearest German rival, Dresdner Bank, but is still under 27 per cent of the size of Citigroup. Only high market capitalisation act as a buffer against hostile bids and here German companies are weak. This leads commentators to argue that German corporations stand on the edge of a swathe of hostile takeovers by foreign companies (*Wirtschaftswoche*, 7/10.2.00). And, since eight out of the ten largest companies in each sector are American, weight is lent to the dominance of the Anglo-American corporate model of *shareholder* value.

Under-capitalisation is a weakness which stems from the corporatist and legal structures of *Modell Deutschland*. The largest German companies have, historically, had one house bank which is represented on the Supervisory Board and which hold the proxy voting rights for numerous small shareholders. There are several features of this *stakeholder* system:

- Consensus voting at a supervisory level and representation of stakeholder interests (as opposed to shareholder interests) both within and outside the firm (*Mitbestimmungsgesetz*).
- Tight delineations of responsibility and careful transfer of information between levels in the organisational hierarchy, and, critically, between interest groups in the organisation (*Betriebsverfassungsgesetz*).
- Supervisory representation and proxy-voting on behalf of small shareholders (*Aktiengesetz* and *Mitbestimmungsgesetz*).
- Willingness of external or quasi-external stakeholders (banking consortia or the supervisory board) to assume control in times of 'crisis' (for example during threats from hostile takeovers).
- Interlocking patterns of company directorships and representation on external governmental bodies (for example, determining the content of training and national level pay negotiations).

The Vodafone–Airtouch takeover of Mannesmann demonstrated the apparent weakness of this stakeholder system. There was no banking consortium offering to help, the interventions from Gerhard Schröder proved fruitless and, in the end, not even Mannesmann's very public appeal to its own shareholders, could keep the company 'German'.

So perhaps the concern about the viability of German corporatism is justified. In the 1980s the model of stakeholder value was much praised as a means of generating long-termism and security (Prais 1982; Lane 1989; Hutton 1995). By the end of the 1990s however, the equity-based capitalism of the Anglo-American model dominates. Put simplistically, dividends to shareholders and high market capitalisation have taken

Table 7.1 **Market capitalisation in billion euro of the world's largest companies in ten key sectors**

German Company and sector	*German company's market valuation*	*Rank in world*	*Sector leader*	*Sector leader's market valuation*
Automotive				
Daimler–Chrysler	68.0	2	Toyota (J)	176.3
BMW	16.0	7		
Volkswagen	14.4	8		
Finance				
Deutsche Bank	50.0	10	Citigroup (USA)	188.3
Dresdner Bank	25.8	26		
Hypo Vereinsbank	23.3	27		
Commerzbank	16.3	42		
Electronincs				
Siemens	98.1	2	General Electric (USA)	473.8
Retail				
Metro	12.3	16	Wal-Mart (USA)	256.3
Karstadt	3.8	41		
Media				
Springer	4.3	69	AOL/Time Warner (USA)	232.7
Pharmaceuticals/Chemicals				
Aventis	44.7	16	Pfizer/Warner Lambert (USA)	224.3
Bayer	29.9	17		
BASF	26.4	18		
Software				
SAP	75.9	5	Microsoft (USA)	562.0
Steel				
Thyssen–Krupp	14.5	4	Alcoa Reynolds (USA)	30.6
Telecommunications				
Deutsche Telekom	249.9	3	NTT CoDoMo (J)	346.8
Insurance				
Allianz	82.3	2	AIG (USA)	159.3
Münchener Bank	50.5	4		

Source: Derived from *Wirtschaftswoche*, 7. 10 Feb. 2000 pp. 50–3.

precedence over the more complex interests of stakeholders. Workers are encouraged to take responsibility over their own tasks instead of relying on unions to represent their interests. New technology and working practices have enabled companies to pass autonomy down to task-based operational groups with a focus on continuously improving the quality of the product and of their own working environment (Bessant *et al.* 1994; Harding 1996). Total quality is paramount in the interest of serving the needs of customers and shareholders across the globe (Reich 1995). Under these circumstances, then, the stakeholder model of German corporatism is, at best, severely challenged and, at worst, defunct.

It would, however, be simplistic indeed, to decry the German model on the basis of one hostile takeover, albeit a high profile one. Indeed, Mannesmann was 80 per cent owned by overseas shareholdings anyway. In 1995 there were no German companies in the world's top 25 largest companies by market capitalisation. Now there are 13. The meteoric growth of the software company SAP has astonished even the sternest critics of the German model. Germany now has its highest ever rate of new business start-ups, especially in Information and Communications Technology (ICT) and biotechnology. So is German corporatism dead, is it metamorphosing into something new or is it merely adapting to the new competitive pressures of the global economy?

It is the purpose of this chapter to try and shed some light on the process of change through which *Modell Deutschland* is now going. It begins with a discussion of the key features of the model and argues that its dynamic has to be understood on two levels – first in terms of the micro-organisational structures that affect company decision-making and second in terms of the macro-institutional structures which are the essence of the inter-connectivities between actors in the German system. These are legally constituted structures as well as quasi-coordination which has evolved through custom and practice. Commonly, flaws in the model are attributed to inherent weaknesses in the industrial relations system which is a product of co-determination. However, the co-determination law itself governs much more than worker representation. It is argued, therefore, that taking too narrow a perspective on the nature of the German model or its adaptiveness to change leads to misleading conclusions.

Next we examine Germany's capacity to produce change since this is the essence of its adaptiveness. It argues that the current pressures are, in terms of the strength of their impact, no stronger than the pressures to introduce new technologies during the 1980s. In the sense that German industrial society has adapted to change in the past, then, it is inappropriate to use the term, 'model' since this implies a degree of rigidity which is not historically proven to exist. The section concludes, therefore with a critique of the suggestion that the systemic dynamic for change comes from appropriate incentivisation. Rather, it argues, this systemic dynamic in Germany emanates from its networked and collective nature.

This is developed finally by a more detailed analysis of the emerging start-up sector in Germany. On the basis of a case study of venture capital structures in the Cologne area (and supported by evidence from policy documentation), it argues that both the financial and employment systems have proved themselves capable of appropriate adaptation without fundamentally under-mining the corporate structures of its industrial society.

The argument propounded here, then, is that German corporatism is not dead, nor is it changing into something unrecognisably different. Viewed historically, the adaptive strengths of the system are proven. There is evidence to suggest that the system has to change, and the data provided at the outset of this chapter lend support to that contention. However, the issue of whether or not the system has to change is, in many senses, immaterial in comparison to the question of how it is changing now and how it has changed in the past. It is to this that the remainder of the chapter turns now.

The features of the German system[1]

The historical base

By definition, then, '*Modell Deutschland*' is a system. If conclusions about '*Standort Deutschland*' are to be reached, then the viability of the whole system over time has to be assessed. As the brief discussion of the legal basis of German corporatism above has aimed to demonstrate, it is an incomplete picture that illustrates the performance of an individual feature at any one point in time. Rather, these individual components have evolved into a system through history. While it is common to view *Modell Deutschland* as the product of the immediate post-war years, this hides the origins of the German *system*: For example:

- *Education and training can be traced back to the thirteenth Century* (Milward and Saul 1979). This includes the system of corporate funding for university professorships which formed the basis of the technology transfer system.

- *Collaborative, partnership and applied research is characteristic of the German innovation system.* For example, Robert Bosch GmbH was founded in the nineteenth century on research principles. Its first product was a starter motor which combined basic scientific knowledge with its commercial application (Harding 1995). Similarly, the Fraunhofer Gesellschaft, the bastion of applied research in post-war Germany takes its ideology from Joseph Fraunhofer, an applied researcher and entrepreneur who developed glass manufacturing techniques using sophisticated optical equipment as early as the first quarter of the nineteenth century (Fraunhofer Gesellschaft 1997).
- *The financial system* has its origins in the eighteenth century when the Deutsche Bank had been established as the housebank of the newly founded Siemens. By 1903 Hilferding noted that the six big Berlin banks controlled 751 positions on Boards of Directors of leading companies (Hilferding, 1981, see also Lenin, 1982, Scott 1997, Shonfeld 1969). The system of inter-locking directorships has characterised the system of capital mobilization and, in the post-war period has been admired as creating the long-term strategic perspective inherent to the German system.

  Both the political model of the social market economy and one of its principal components, the system of industrial relations, were built on pre-Weimar structures. Codetermination is visible in companies before the First World War, and information and communications structures, date back to the 1920s (Augsdorfer and Harding 1996). The liberal tradition of the post-war social market economy can actually be traced back to the 'Paulskirche' constitution of 1849 which was more politically liberal than the 1871 constitution. 'Instead of liberalizing the economy, industrialization gives rise in Germany to a highly organised economic society based on the play of public and private powers and counter-balances' (Broyer 1996).

The German system, which gave rise to the post-war 'model' has, then, to be viewed within its historical context. In so doing, it can be seen that the post-war 'economic miracle' of German corporatism and of which commentators have heralded the end, was not the first economic miracle worked by the German social market economy. A miracle of equal, if not greater, proportions had been worked during the 'catch-up' phase of German industrialisation during the nineteenth century. Arguably, the first and second economic miracles were worked on the basis of very similar institutional structures. Representation of strong interest groups in finance, industrial relations, education and training and research at a corporate and policy formulation level is characteristic of the German system. And organisation and inter-locking relationships were integral to German economic, social and industrial development even before the 1871 constitution (Scott 1997). The major adaptation of the post-war period was the formalisation of the 'social market' apex to the model. Thus, the system has adapted previously and only by recognising this is it possible to understand the prospects for adaptation in the future.

The German system has evolved to produce and support a highly integrated, adaptive and, crictically, competitive, industrial economy. This economy has remained competitive in international markets despite the assimilation of the large but under-developed economy of Eastern Germany. The system can only be criticised first, if it is not producing competitive companies and second, if it is it not reproducing its historically based strengths in innovation and high technology. So it is necessary to investigate the context in which companies operate, at a corporate, strategic level and at a national institutional level in order to assess how the process of change affects the whole system and, hence, companies who are supported by that system.

The micro system: the corporate context

The *Mitbestimmungsgesetz* of 1976 is commonly viewed as the definition of workers' rights to equal representation at a supervisory board level in all companies over 500 employees[2]. It is the *Betriebsverfassungsgesetz* that further defines the right for workers to be represented at a works council (*Betriebsrat*) level in all companies over 20 employees. A wider discussion of these acts goes beyond the scope of this paper. However, they do merit some mention here simply because it is through these acts that the inter-connectivity between macro-level policy-makers and micro-level actors is effected.

The reason for this inter-connectivity is defined in the laws themselves. German companies formulate strategies, short term and long term, within the framework illustrated in figure 7.1 which is the organisational structure of large German companies under the *Aktiengesetz*, the *Mitbestimmungsgesetz* and the *Betriebsverfassungsgesetz*. Under this system, management, workers and the interests of capital are represented in roughly equal proportions on the supervisory board of the company. The function of the supervisory board is to oversee activities of the company so that, on a day to day basis, it has little to do with the operations of the company. However, it does have the power to appoint members of the executive board. Thus in times of crisis, its potential power is significant (Kittner 1982). It receives information via representatives from the trade unions, from management, from the house bank and from major shareholders.

It is not the purpose of this paper to discuss the relative power of individual actors nor to discuss the efficacy with which information flows within this structure. However, two factors are of critical relevance to the discussion about the German system generally. First, as is clear from the

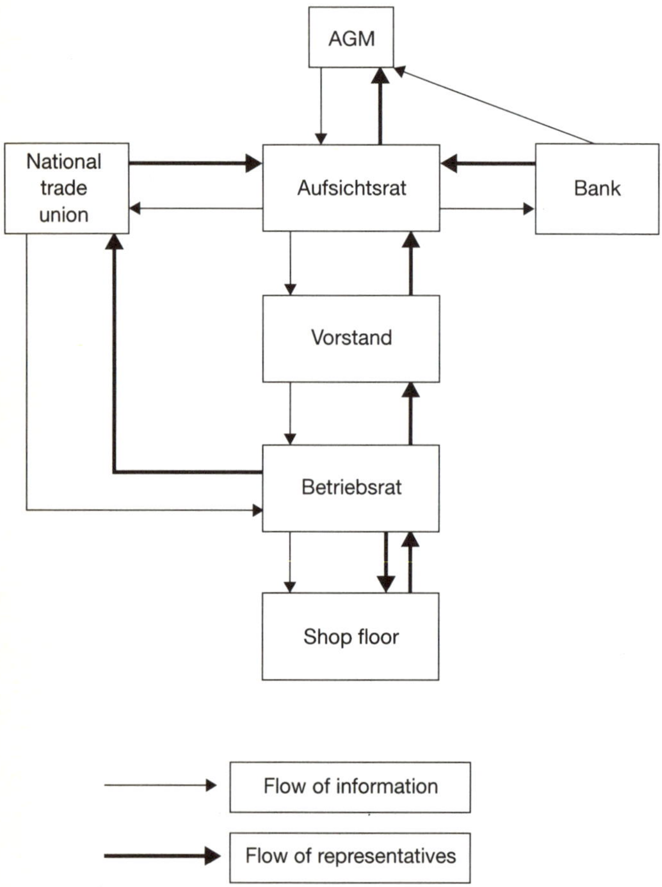

Figure 7.1 **The micro-system: the corporate context**

arrows in figure 7.1, there are strong interconnections between the interests of finance, management and capital through this system that extend down to the shop floor of the company from the national structures of trade unions, shareholders and banks. Representatives and information are exchanged between the supervisory board of a company, its house bank and its major shareholders. The effect of this is the inter-locking directorships for which Germany is renowned.[3] Further, the house bank has influence on the voting patterns of small shareholders through the proxy-voting system.[4] Information and representatives are further exchanged between the works council, the shop floor and the national trade union, further broadening the extent of interconnectivity at least passively.

Second, any discussion of either the relationship between management and employees or the relationship between management and capital within German companies has to take into account the interests of other parties, as they are closely interdependent through the industrial relations system. For example, if German companies make increasing use of short-term, external equity-based finance through international markets, this has the potential to alter the role of the supervisory board both in terms of the relationship between management and the house bank *and* in terms of the balance of power between representatives of labour and capital.

The 'macro' system: the institutional context

The inter-relationships are not limited to the structure of co-determination or inter-locking directorships, however. Trade unions, business and finance are all involved in policy formulation through national committee membership. The micro-level system illustrated above represents the daily environment in which companies operate. At a macro-environmental level, a complex web of institutions forms a support network for companies to ensure, for example the supply of a well trained and educated work force, applied technology research, access to finance and stable, non-confrontational industrial relations. This sophisticated 'factor' environment has long been admired as contributing to Germany's post-war economic miracle and creating its domestic competitive advantage. It can be broadly illustrated as in figure 7.2.

While the model is highly stylised, like that presented in figure 7.1, it highlights a number of important issues:

- The financial system has historically supported German companies in two ways: first, through aggressive policies of the Bundesbank to keep

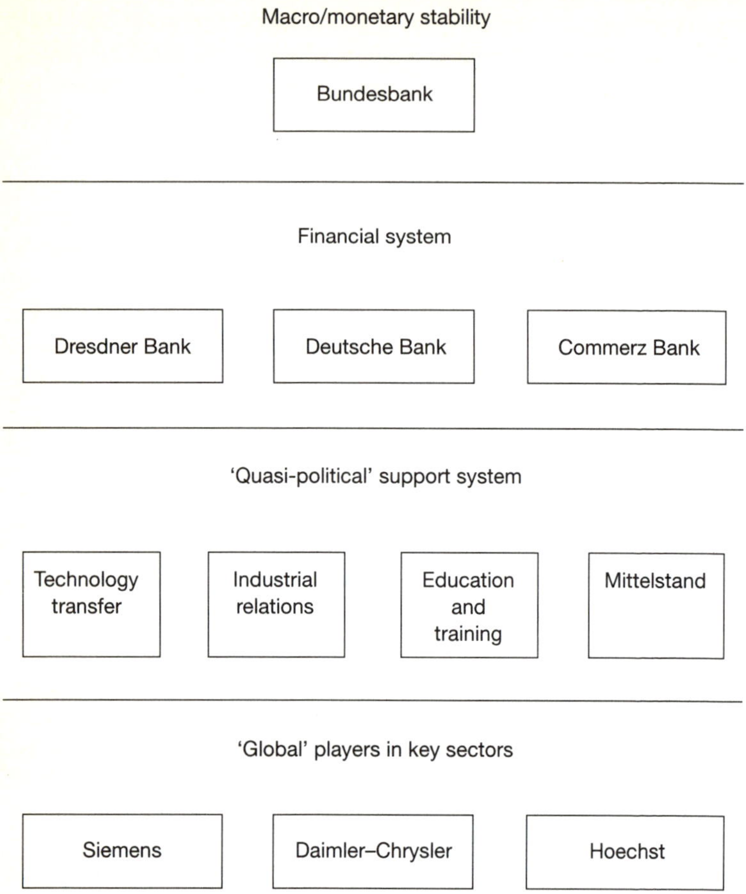

Figure 7.2 **The macro-system: the institutional context**

interest rates low and the value of the Deutschmark at a level to ensure German goods are competitive internationally and domestically (Boltho 1982). Second, the largest, 'universal' banks are the long-term financiers, particularly of big business, as well as shareholders and managers of shareholder accounts. This arguably has provided German industry with a financial security which has allowed its companies to make long-term strategic decisions rather than be concerned about short-term return to shareholders.

- The network of 'para-political' organisations supplying companies with factors of production have a significant role in policy implementation *and* policy formulation. These organisations are all inter-linked with one another: for example, universities and Fachhochschulen are central to the innovation system as well as to the education system. The Mittelstand is placed in the section of factor supply in that it is integral to the innovation system and is similarly linked to large companies through the supply chain.
- The 'global' companies selected here represent the 'household name' companies that straddle the five sectors in which Germany has historical innovative and competitive strength internationally: electronics, automobiles, mechanical engineering, pharmaceuticals. The selected companies are those, following Cantwell and Harding (1998)[5] that have significant overseas R&D operations as well as substantial sales and productive capacity outside of Germany.

The purpose of these models is to illustrate the relationships between actors within the German system and their interface with the micro-environment in which companies operate. It is important to view the models as historically derived: they are a valid representation of the system that has evolved through industrialisation and post-war reconstruction, and they represent the structure that has provided Germany with its competitive advantage in high quality incremental innovation. As will be argued below, the challenge of the global era is to retain the strengths of the system while adapting to a new economic order, or paradigm.

Change and Corporate Germany – An inflexible model or a driver of change?

As is clear by taking the historical perspective outlined above, German industrial society and, hence, its institutions have developed according to a collaborative and networked pattern. This has resulted in the laws and structures that are commonly termed, '*Modell Deutschland*', of which co-determination is an important part. But the pattern of change itself cannot be defined so easily. Like all evolutionary processes, the change itself is neither regular nor definable and is affected by those external forces (for example, massive political upheavals or shifts in technological paradigm) which require particular changes to happen.

Discussion about co-determination has altered. In the 1970s argument centred around the model itself and making it work effectively to represent all stakeholders in Germany's industrial society. By the 1980s discussion had shifted somewhat to an examination of the appropriateness of the model it represented in relation to the introduction of new technology. By the end of the 1990s the altogether more fatalistic discussion was about co-determination in its widest sense as a symbol of *Modell Deutschland* and hence, centred around its capacity to produce a globally competitive economy. This shift in emphasis, represents a shift in the definition of co-determination itself – from a narrow definition of representation of worker rights to a very broad concept which encompasses, indeed embodies, all of the institutional structures of 'corporate' Germany. This move, from a model of social integration to a model of economic performance, is at the heart of the *Standortdebatte*.

Taking the broadest possible definition, then, and assuming that *Mitbestimmung* is a historical construct, this leads to some inevitable questions about co-determination. Loosely these are:

- *What are the direct effects of co-determination on industrial decision-making?* Since co-determination is deeply embedded in the complexities of German industrial society, as a by-product of historical development, its direct impact on companies is hard to measure. However, with hind-sight and on a case study format, it is possible to illustrate that its consensus basis does have a positive enabling effect on company decision-making (for more detail see Sorge 1999).
- *What impact does co-determination have as a part of a more complex industrial 'system'?* Germany does not have the highest levels of profitability or, as was shown earlier in the chapter, the highest levels of equity and market capitalisation in the world. However, it does have high labour productivity which is a direct consequence of effective worker representation in the determination and provision of education and training. This is coordinated through nationally based committees to meet the needs of manufacturing companies and, while this 'dual system' has been criticised for its relative slowness in providing adequate training for hi-tech, the fact remains that German manufacturing companies can rely on a highly skilled and motivated work force which still continues to provide a substantial competitive advantage in international markets.
- *How valid are the current, widespread criticisms and doubts about codetermination?* Critics of the German model all too frequently regard co-determination as simply a structure for worker representation. Here, indeed, it has its weaknesses and may seem to produce unwieldy deci-

sion-making processes and inflexible labour markets. But, as has already been argued, this is erroneous since it does not take into account the complexities of codetermination itself and, indeed, of its relation with the other legal structures in Germany. This does not imply that some criticisms do not have their validity. German companies have been relatively slow to adopt the decentralised labour relations of total quality management, arguing instead that these structures are embedded through a requirement for work place suggestion schemes (Augsdorfer and Harding 1995), although there is strong case study evidence to suggest that this is changing. Perhaps more worrying is the accusation that the system has failed to provide for full employment, as witnessed by current high levels of unemployment. Here, perhaps, the argument in favour of looking at the macro coordination of government policies, trade unions and employers are the strongest since it is in that interface that the real difficulties lie.

- *What future does co-determination have?* Under decentralised working patterns, vertical disintegration and an era of low labour costs and global markets the deficits of the co-determination structure as a means of ensuring the collective affluence of Germany seem limited. Individualism is paramount and this appears to be counter-intuitive under the current model of codetermination. But, and this is critical, the structures have to be seen in the context of the rest of corporate Germany, including the *Betriebsverfassungsgesetz* and the *Aktiengesetz.* It may be that through changes in these laws, the collaborative essence of codetermination can be sustained while introducing decentralised, autonomous and flexible decision-making structures.

This last point, then takes us to the core of the problem. German social and economic history is a product of the duality of perceived best practice elsewhere and the internal drive to catch up with that best practice. Understanding Germany as a 'model' implies that the structures cannot be changed. This is historically proven to be false. Indeed, the capacity to produce competitive change has been a remarkable feature of the country's turbulent political and economic development.

The interesting question, then, is about the drive behind this 'dualism' that is the motor of change in Germany. Soskice's seminal work on national innovation systems (Soskice 1994) develops the contention that the adaptive and incremental nature of change emanates from the lack of incentive structures which promote radical innovation and entrepreneurial behaviour. He conducts a cross country study of America, the

UK, Japan and Germany. America and the UK, he argues, fall into a category of 'liberal market economies' (often termed, the Anglo-Saxon model). Here, trade unionism is weak, training is outside the private sector and companies have an 'arms-length' relationship with their owners and with banks. This provides a degree of flexibility, as well as *individualistic* incentive structures which favour radical innovations and change. Technology transfer is through industrial associations (often in the private sector) which have profit as their primary motivation (Soskice 1994: 273). In contrast, he argues, 'coordinated market economies', which include Germany, are characterised by organised training (with strong employer involvement), cooperative trade unions (at macro-pay bargaining and micro-strategic decision-making levels) and long term relations with banks. Technology transfer is through quasi-coordinated public and private sector organisations which are incentivised through contracts rather than a specific profit motive. Collective incentives are strong in terms of higher standards of living, but broadly summarised, this model tends to favour incremental rather than radical change.

So, the key difference, according to Soskice, is that radical innovations come from individual rather than collective behaviour and that the German model generates the latter. If this is the case it leads to a rather pessimistic view of the future of its institutional structures. As Casper *et al.* argue:

> High risk, high-return 'blockbuster' products are unlikely to be created from the German pattern of industrial and financial organisation. It is difficult for German firms to quickly move in and out of markets characterised by rapidly evolving technologies. Since most employment contracts are unlimited, top managers of German firms must think twice before creating new competencies in high-risk areas, for cutting assets is difficult. Similarly, it is difficult for German firms to create the high-powered performance incentives for managers, unilateral decision-making structures and opportunities for rapid career advancement because the organisational structures go against the logic of the established institutional framework and would risk alienating important long-term stakeholders to the firm ... Many of the traditional and institutional constraints as well as the small labour market for mid-career scientists and technicians continue to hamper the efforts of German high-tech start-ups. These constraints limit the ability of start-up companies to move quickly into new fields as these firms start to grow. (Casper *et al.* 1999: 12).

If competitiveness is defined by the capacity of a system to produce radical innovations, then the structures within Germany appear inadequate (see also Mason and Wagner 1999).

We argue, however, that this is a limited argument on two grounds. First, it assumes that the 'model' that produces the institutional structures of an economy is fixed. This approach uses the tools of neo-classical economics, in particular, incentivisation through the profit motive, to present a picture of rigidity and unadaptiveness which simply reflects its comparative static methodology. We contend it is less interesting to look at the model, since this necessarily implies rigidity, than it is to look at the process of adaptation to change and the extent to which these are determined by the industrial *system* of a particular nation state. Three aspects of the development of the German financial system in the nineteenth century serve as pertinent examples of change here:

> A suitable system which combined both private and equity capital with State loan finance was visible as early as 1845, both through actual loans to support priority areas (for example to Siemens to support electro-mechanics which had military applications) and through participation in financial institutions that had a particular focus on facilitating development. Large bank lending was as a 'last resort' when all alternative methods of financing had been exhausted. (Milward and Saul 1979: 421)

Laws developed to complement developments in the financing of innovations and of entrepreneurs. Thus, the *simultane Gründung*, for example, provided a legal framework whereby a bank could put 'capital into the enterprise and then sell off shares over the counter when the company was off the ground' (Milward and Saul 1979: 425).[6] As Milward and Saul argue,

> The development of the German banking system has to be seen, not as the sudden escape of bourgeois capitalism from the control of reactionary governments leading to a tremendous onward leap in the process of economic development, *but as a perfectly normal evolution of a mode of thought and practice already created in the first half of the (19th) Century. What changed was not the supply of capital but the demand for it as the availability of resources and the scale of technology both changed.* (Milward and Saul 1979: 418, emphasis added)

Second, we maintain that the use of individual incentivistion as a driver for radical innovation is itself limiting in the German case. Under Anglo-Saxon institutional structures, individualism is embedded and, hence, is the means for generating change. This does not mean, however, that the German economy is incapable of producing high-risk entrepreneurial and innovative behaviour. Indeed, we would argue that the networked and *collective* nature of German industrial society is capable of producing radical innovation in the twenty-first century at a rate at least equal to if not greater than that in the much-praised Anglo-American system. This is based on an assumption that the process of change is more interesting than the nature of the institutions themselves. Although this is more difficult to measure in terms of rigorous economic criteria, the weight of historical evidence suggests that this is a fruitful avenue of enquiry.

This confidence is based on both data and on case study evidence which is explored in greater detail in this section. If, as has been suggested above, competitiveness is measured in terms of the capacity of a system to produce radically innovative and entrepreneurial behaviour, then we need to produce evidence that this is indeed what is happening within the German system. The data presented in tables 7.2 and 7.3 therefore should not be looked at in terms of absolute or even relative figures in relation to other countries. Since Germany has been in 'catch-up' mode throughout the 1990s, this is misleading. Rather, the rates of change in each of the indicators should be examined as this give an idea of the of the adaptive capacity of the system.

Seed-corn/start-up finance in Germany has grown exponentially since 1994 as table 7.2 demonstrates and Germany's *Neuer Markt* (technology stock market) has seen its index rise over 700 per cent (higher than the European technology market EASDAQ, or the technology markets in France, Germany or Britain). While the overall level of seed-corn funding is low relative, say to Britain or America, Germany has the second-largest venture capital sector in Europe (after Britain) and it is growing at the fastest rate in Europe (Harding 1999b).

Table 7.2 **Seed-corn and early-stage finance in Germany, 1994–99**

	1994	*1995*	*1996*	*1997*	*1998*	*1999*
Level of seed-corn early stage finance (million DM)	180	175	190	400	900	1600

Source: der Spiegel, 7/2000.

Table 7.2 suggests that there has been a rapid expansion in funding for small, high-growth companies. The business angel market is flourishing;

Table 7.3 **Comparative indicators of innovativeness in biotechnology across Germany, France, the UK and the US**

	Growth in venture capital investments (1996–97)	*Average % increase in world's publication oputput*[a]	*US patent applications (1990–98)*[b]
US	n/a	–0.64	48,845
UK	+0.3	0.93	3636
Germany	+55.3	3.25	4801
France	+34.5	2.84	1985

Source: Derived from Crowther *et al.* 1999.
Notes: [a] Averaged across four sectors: medicing, biomedical, biology and engineering. [b] Total across four related fields; genetic engineering, molecular biology and microbiology, drugs and multicellular living organisms.

traditional banks, like the KfW and the Kreissparkassen, have taken on the role as start-up financiers for regionally based projects and this is supported by national-level policies to provide mentoring and finance to potential start-up companies through the Bundesministerium für Bildung und Forschung (BMBF) and the Bundesministerium für Wirtschaft (BMWi). As the weekly reporting of new company flotations in *Wirtschaftswoche* demonstrates, these largely, although not exclusively, are technology based. What is remarkable in the system as it is developing is the sophisticated leverage from seed-capital financing through to eventual flotation which allows companies to realise their high growth potential (Harding 1999b).

It is in the field of radical innovations, however, that criticisms of the German model are most frequently voiced. Particularly in the areas of ITC and biotechnology the structures of the system are seen as rigid and unsupportive of business needs in competitive international markets. It is thus worth dwelling for a while on one of these areas, biotechnology, in order to gain a picture of the extent to which radical innovations are possible within Germany. This focus is justified since in contrast to other technology intensive industries, 'commercial advance in biotech relies still on the interaction of the public and private sectors due to the early maturity stage of this technology' (Pfirmann and Feldman 1998). In other words, governments and technology transfer centres (including universities) have to work with private-sector organisations in order to move the technology forward. Biotechnology is thus a test case for the durability of the partnership/collaborative nature of the German system.

Table 7.3 provides some comparative data for biotechnology indicators in comparison with the US, the UK and France. The indicators are selected on the following grounds:

- *Venture capital investments*: gives indication of levels of biotech start-ups and access to 'new' financing methods.
- *Increase in world's publications*: acts as a proxy for path-breaking 'blue-sky research'.
- *US patents*: acts as a proxy for innovation and commercial potential.

Clearly Europe generally is a long way behind the United States in terms of key indicators of innovativeness. However, Germany has, largely through a huge expansion in biotechnology research start-up activity, overtaken the UK as Europe's leading player. Table 7.3 shows that the level of research in biotechnology in Germany is high and, critically, that the potential for commercialisation is also high, as evidenced by the level of venture capital investment.

Crowther *et al.*'s work demonstrates remarkably weak links between the academic base in universities and the commercialisation of biotechnology (Crowther *et al.* 1999: 22). This may emanate from weaknesses in the patenting and intellectual property rights regimes governing university spin-outs rather than an intrinsic weakness in the technology transfer system (Schmoch 1998). But perhaps of even more interest is the extent to which biotechnology research in Germany is increasingly funded by corporate venturing (in other words, large firms purchasing an equity stake in small, research-based start ups). Germany's largest pharmaceuticals companies, like Bayer, Hoechst and BASF, use this innovation mechanism of reducing, even externalising, the risks attached to basic science inherent in conducting the research 'in house'.

Finally, a short case study, of an innovation incubator, presents an even richer picture of how large and small companies, banks and venture capitalists and public and private sector partners (including universities and technology transfer organisations) have worked together. Working under the government's 'Innoregio'[7] programme and with the involvement of private sector companies, the area around Cologne has been regenerated from its manufacturing base to an innovation centre. The Cologne Sparkasse has provided seed-corn and start-up finance as well as mentoring and small business support to 18 new firms in the area in biotechnology, genetics, ICT and new materials since 1997. The Bergisch Gladbach technology park accommodates these start-up firms and is designed to maximise synergies and technology transfer between the companies based there. From the original 150 companies and 1,700 jobs that were provided in 1996, a further 50 companies have spun out and another 500 jobs have been created. Large companies have strong links with the park in order to facilitate their own spin-out, technology transfer and corporate venturing activities. The Rheinische Hochschule für Technik und Wissenschaft runs competitions for the best start-up ideas and provides access to start-up capital financiers. Finally, and perhaps most interestingly as a measure of flexible corporatism, the finance director of the venture capital arm of the Cologne Sparkasse has become conversant as a technical specialist in technology areas, particularly biotechnology and biomedics. As he cheerfully said, 'I'm much more than a banker now!' (RH interviews December 1999).

What those who criticise the inability of Germany to produce more radical innovation fail to recognise is that any innovation is a long-term process, which at the beginning is more radical and, at later stages of diffusion, more piecemeal. For innovation to be macro-economically productive, it requires diffusion and spread. What Germany has been better at is to diffuse an innovation once it is beyond the more elementary stages, achieve high penetration and generate benefits through customised and piecemeal continuous adaptation (Sorge 1999). On that basis, it has won market shares from competitors from countries which had been earlier pioneers. This is a consistent feature of industrial history, and there is no reason why it should not repeat itself again now, in the case of biotechnology. German-type institutional structures may even persist and be reinforced although shareholder capitalism and richer equity are being adopted. To see this in operation, we only need to take a glimpse at Switzerland, which has had high equity/debt ratios, very different from Germany, for a long time. Such niceties are important for the future but have been curiously overlooked in many more sweeping contributions.

Concluding remarks

This chapter has attempted to shift the discussion of the future of the German corporatism away from inflammatory statements about its durability and towards a systematic discussion of its *adaptive* potential.

Looking at the model from the perspective of co-determination and the rigidities inherent in large company decision-making, it has been argued, is misleading because it does not provide a true picture of the dynamic for change that drives the economy. This dynamic is commonly misunderstood as being relatively slow moving and incremental in nature.

This, as the argument at the outset of the chapter outlined, has resulted in commentators predicting the demise of the institutions of German capitalism for two principal reasons:

- Labour market inflexibility which produces high labour costs and high unemployment.
- Under-capitalisation of the largest German firms which renders them prone to hostile takeover.

Both are seen by critics as being a product of the co-determination system and its interface with the complex legal and administrative structures of *Modell Deutschland.*

However, we have argued here that the reason that the corporate system is seen as being slow is because of the focus on the model itself rather than on its adaptive capacity. The evidence presented here suggests a degree of change which, far from de-constructing the model in favour of an individualistic Anglo-Saxon paradigm, is including individualism as part of its collective nature. Thus, for example, there is scope for entrepreneurial behaviour and radical innovation. And this is supported by a traditional technology transfer and policy structure which has demonstrated a remarkable capacity to incorporate 'new' structures like venture capital without undermining old ones.

On the basis of a better historical appreciation, it even turns out that the challenge now facing Germany is not that radically new. Certainly as far as technical and commercial competitiveness of enterprises-at-large are concerned – which are different from radical change and innovation – it still has a competitive edge. We would also contest that globalising capital markets override any other markets. Maybe international investors will invest in German companies precisely because they function within a German context, if they are not doing it for short-term speculative reasons.

Notes

1 The next two sections are derived from earlier work by the authors. For more detail, see Sorge, A. (1999): 'Mitbestimmung, Arbeitsorganisation und Tech-

nikanwendung' in Streek, W. and Kluge, N. (eds) *Mitbestimmung in Deutschland: Tradition und Effizienz.* Frankfurt: Kommission Mitbestimmung, Bertelsmann Stiftung, Hans-Böckler Stiftung, Campus Verlag. Harding, R. (1999a): 'Standort Deutschland: An End to the Economic Miracle?' *German Politics*, April, 1999.

2 For a full discussion of the laws governing organisational structure see, Bamberg, U., Dzielack, W., Hindrichs, W. and Martens, J. (1984): *Praxis der Unternehmensmitbestimmunung nach dem Mitbestimmungsgesetz.* Düsseldorf: Hans-Böckler Stiftung; or Kittner, M. (1982): *Mitbestimmung im Unternehmung und Betrieb* Düsseldorf: Hans-Böckler Stiftung.

3 For a Sociological perspective on this see Scott (1997). A business perspective on the same issue is given by Randelsome, (1994): *The Business Culture in Germany: Portrait of a Powerhouse.* London: Butterworth-Heinemann.

4 Whereby the house bank holds the shares of small shareholders and acts on their behalf.

5 Cantwell and Harding (1998) conduct an analysis of patenting activity of the largest German companies in order to establish the extent to which their technological and research operations are conducted on a 'global' basis. Strong sectoral dominance in electronics, automobiles and chemicals/pharmaceuticals is identified by their study which provides the rationale for the selected companies here.

6 This is sophisticated enabling of venture capital as early as the 19th century!

7 The Innoregio programme is a competition to stimulate innovation and competitiveness in regions across Germany (including the '*neue Länder*'). This competition has been running since April 1999. The best twenty-five were selected in November 1999 – each received grants from the BMBF to implement their innovation strategies.

8

An end to the miracle?

Rebecca Harding and William E. Paterson

Introduction

So where does the material presented in this book leave us? Is Germany in crisis? Will its institutions and structures allow it to compete in the 'global' era? Or will the 'German model' be subsumed into an Anglo-Saxon policy ideal in which markets have precedence over policy?

It is worth dwelling for a while on the central purpose of this book. As the title implies, we set out to look at the *future* potential for the German economy. This future, it has been argued throughout the text, is critically dependent upon its institutional structures and their inherent adaptability to current market conditions. In particular, these institutional structures have historically provided a strong factor base (in terms of high skills and long-term capital) and stability. Recently the long termism and rigidity of these institutional frameworks has been regarded as a hindrance to German competitiveness. But it is our contention that the pervasiveness of these institutions through the sophisticated web of networks, public–private sector partnerships and governance structures provides a depth of resource to policy-makers and industrialists alike that is scarcely rivalled elsewhere.

We have looked at an economy which has undergone a series of profound exogenous shocks. It was a late-comer to industrialisation, yet had caught up, indeed overtaken, Britain by the turn of the twentieth century. This catch-up process was built on sophisticated and, surprisingly post-industrial, coordinated structures, particularly of finance. As was discussed by Harding and Sorge in chapter 7, there were structures for 'modern' capital formation as early as 1845 inherent in legislation to support equity stakes by banks in start-up firms. Thus, the manufacturing sectors largely developed within the institutional structures of bank-based finance readily associated with *Modell Deutschland.* Alongside, however, the highly successful and, at its inception globally dominant, chemical industry was funded out of its own equity (*Eigenkapital*) (Grant *et al.* 1988).

Similarly, after the destruction of two world wars, the German economy was re-moulded, albeit under Allied guidance, into familiar forms and institutional networks (Cusack 1997, Broyer 1996). The historical routes of the dual system of education and training, for example, can be found in the thirteenth century while co-determination structures can be found in pre-Weimar Germany (Harding 1999a). New structures were developed alongside those that had stood the test of time.

And now Germany faces more shocks – unification and globalisation in particular. The challenges now are to be dynamic, to innovate and to be market responsive. Neo-classical economics would tell us that these are the domain of small business – the rigid institutional structures are no longer appropriate. The key words for policy are 'flexibility', 'knowledge-based economy' and 'entrepreneurial culture' – seemingly anathema to the corporatist roots of the German economy.

So why are we so positive? What right do we as 'outsiders' have to be optimistic about the future of the German economy?

Let us start with re-examining the features of the 'global' era and mapping them against the institutional structures that we have covered in this book, as illustrated in table 8.1.

Table 8.1 **A map of German institutional structures against the imperatives for competitiveness in the global era**

Feature of the 'global era'	*German institutional structures*
Importance of networks	Dominance of networks, partnerships and collective behaviour in all areas of system
Centrality of technology	Technology transfer through institutional structures and through 'embeddedness' for example in education and training and criteria for promotion
Need for specialisation	Industrial structures are highly specialised in chemicals, pharmaceuticals, electronics, metal-working and automobiles. Institutional structures reflects this.
Swiftness to market and radical innovations	Policy priorities to enable venture capital to support emerging technologies and start-ups. Competition and collaboration between and within institutional structures. Historically based adaptiveness.

The first three rows of table 8.1 are well-documented as institutional strengths of the German economy. Networks and collaborative partnerships have always dominated, innovation has been a bed-rock of the German economy since it first industrialised and the patterns of industrial development and of internationalisation have centred around five key sectors. As a result, commentators have pointed to weakness in fast-growing technologies such as biotech and IT.

It is the last row that, perhaps, presents the most surprises in the light of this last comment, then. Steps taken in national policy, to biotechnology through the Bioregio programme and to create innovative regions through the Innoregio programmes have, until recently, been under-publicised. But, as Adelberger argues, these do represent a significant leadership role that has been taken by the German government (Adelberger 2000). Development criteria have been set – here biotechnology and innovative regions – and all infrastructures and institutions within the system have been incentivised actively to participate. And, as is indicated, in table 8.1, this adaptiveness is historically based. Examples of priority setting for policy purposes go back to the 1870s textile industry again supported by suitable access to finance, an innovation infrastructure and a well-developed training system (Milward and Saul 1979).

Exogenous shocks

We have not dealt with the assimilation of eastern Germany extensively since our focus has been on Germany's economic performance in a global perspective. It is, however, the single most important exogenous shock that the German economy has undergone since the end of the Second World War and, of course, it is unique to Germany whereas, globalisation and Europeanisation are not. But more recently, a huge amount of attention both from within Germany and outside has concentrated on the fact of unification itself anticipating a Mezzogiorno effect to which Marsh refers in chapter 5. It has not looked at the wider capacity of the West German model to assimilate a sizeable but under-developed economy. That was the purpose here.

It is nevertheless expedient to examine some of the issues in relation to eastern Germany since these have been key policy considerations as well as budgetary constraints on the government for the last ten years. As Pohl argues, economic data show general progress throughout the decade (Pohl 2000). GDP growth in the East in comparison to other transition economies and even to western Germany was significantly higher until mid-1998 when Poland's GDP grew faster. Construction industry growth accounted for an important part of this until the second quarter of 1997 when its output fell significantly because of the relative decline in construction orders after that date. This was compensated for, however, by a general upward trend in manufacturing output.

It is in employment that the burning concerns of the East German economy lie. Since 1996 the work force as declined by 225,000 from 6,725,000 to 6,500,000 and, over the same period, unemployment has risen from 14.8 per cent to 17 per cent (DIW 2000). Table 8.2 shows the impact of this on government employment measures and compares it with West Germany.

Table 8.2 **Numbers participating in labour market initiatives in East and West Germany, 1996–99**

Labour market measure	*Average numbers (000s)*							
	1996		*1997*		*1998*		*1999*	
	West	*East*	*West*	*East*	*West*	*East*	*West*	*East*
Short time working	206	71	133	49	81	34	95	30
Job-creation schemes	70	191	59	154	59	152	70	170
Structural adjustment	6	86	8	80	12	163	15	185
Further training	248	207	201	159	179	149	200	145

Source: DIW 2000.

What is remarkable from these figures is the marked difference between labour market adjustment requirements in the East and West. In eastern Germany there is a heavy concentration of people participating in job creation schemes, structural adjustment programmes and further training. The difference between East and West is most marked in the area of structural adjustment programmes where the figure for the East is substantially higher and the gap is widening across the period under consideration.

These data in themselves only underline well-documented differences between the East and West of Germany. There was, after all, a heavy concentration of out-dated manufacturing industry in the former GDR which employed large numbers of people. It is obvious, therefore, that the data would reflect this 'de-industrialisation' in the East while in the West comparatively few people take either job creation or structural adjustment programmes and elect instead for shorter working hours or retraining.

Perhaps this points to a wider difference between the emerging labour market in the East and existing structures in the West. Pohl reports survey data that depict East Germans as acting proactively when faced with risk and as more 'self-determined' (i.e. less collective) in their decision-making (Pohl 2000). Government policy has certainly used the East as a test-bed for new, market based ideas (DIW September 1998) while the level of recruitment into industrial trade unions in the East is low relative to the West. Additionally, the reality of *Verbandsflucht* (East German small companies and foreign firms selecting not to join cooperative associations) suggests some adaptation of the German model (French 1999).

There is evidence to suggest that the East German economy is beginning to reap benefits from the two-fold focus on entrepreneurial activity and improving the capital stock. First, the region's share of total German industry exports rose to 18 per cent by the end of 1999 and East Germany's share of total German industry turnover rose to 7 per cent in the same period. Second, East Germany's produced goods are beginning to find markets in West Germany. These are in their own right measures of improved competitiveness at a micro level (DIW 2000).

This is not to deny the massive problems that still persist and that must still be dealt with at a policy level by the Berlin government. Transfer payments to the East are still extremely high and consumption as a percentage of GDP remains low. As a result, particularly of low consumption, per capita income in the East is unlikely to grow as rapidly as it did in the period of the construction boom.

A second, and dominating, factor that we cannot gloss over is that of unemployment in the whole of Germany. The figures participating in government schemes, as evidenced in table 8.2, are historically high. While it is possible to attribute some of this at least to the process of de-industrialisation and globalisation which affect all economies in the world, the nagging doubt remains that this could signal deep-seated problems with the institutions of *Modell Deutschland* as Funk argues. Further, for a significant proportion of the population it also weakens the legitimacy of what was an extraordinarily consensus-based system.

In particular, the chapters 2 and 3 showed that there are rigidities in the system. Funk argues that this indicates a need for some form of structural change combined with wage moderation in the west and tax incentivisation to encourage small business start ups. In short, adoption of the flexible labour markets principles of the Anglo-Saxon model. While Timmins was a little more positive about the future for the industrial relations system itself neither chapter concluded that current strategies were sufficient to solve the problems of unemployment.

The strengths and weaknesses in context

There are, then, some major weaknesses in the labour markets of both East and West Germany which present a high profile problem to Gerhard Schröder's administration. In monetary terms this emanates from high unit labour costs, although when productivity is included, *real* unit labour costs have been falling for two years now (DIW 1999–2000). The real root of these weaknesses emanates from the macro-level coordination between policy-makers, industry and worker representatives. In particular, the Alliance for Jobs reflects traditional power relations within the industrial relations system and there has been insufficient reform of the costly welfare system to provide significant motivators for change in the labour market. For the moment at least the Schröder government has failed radically to improve the unemployment statistic and, although demography will ultimately come to the rescue, its effects are, by definition, gradual!

But let us put the problem in perspective. The German 'model' has assimilated a massive and under-developed economy and made macroeconomic errors of judgement in the unification of the two currencies. Yet it is still the third largest exporter in the world, it has had consistently low inflation since 1995, its balance of payments is in massive surplus and its GDP growth is forecast to double between 1999 and 2000. Exports are spurred on by the weakness of the euro which ultimately must lead to higher GDP while the balance of payments remains in surplus. If, and when, the euro increases in value, many of its competitors will be wiped out. Further, Germany is now Europe's leading biotechnology innovator and is its fastest growing venture capital market. The company 3i, Europe's largest venture capital business, has just bought Germany's Technology Holdings and has substantially increased its base and cooperation with the government in order to position itself for the anticipated expansion in investment opportunities. Indeed, as a senior official at the EU said, 'One of the reasons why venture capital investments appear so high in Britain is because of the large numbers of funds that invest in German companies without having a base there.'

What future is there for '*Modell Deutschland*'?

Globalisation affects all nation-states of the world, not just Germany. This is a dimension which is often missed, glossed over or ignored in the debate about the future of the German model. Our view is that the German system can adapt while maintaining its core elements. Additionally, as Amoore argues in chapter 4, it is assumed that globalisation will produce a convergence around the Anglo-Saxon model, yet evidence suggests the contrary. As Marsh argues in his chapter, Germany will not undergo a major crisis. Few seriously question the ability of Germany's to compete in the long term or, indeed, of its politicians to formulate and implement policies that maintain the expected high standards of living. Indeed, in comparison with the UK, the micro-structures and micro-level industrial policies are remarkably strong. Germany's economy produced SAP, but where is the next British Microsoft coming from?

But some degree of change is inevitable, as it has been throughout the centuries of modernisation. The key question then, is what changes will come about from this latest period of change?

Despite its failures in labour market reform, the state has learned new tricks. It has learned to stimulate markets through incentives in addition to providing coordination and mentoring structures. It has learned to support entrepreneurial behaviour and innovation while simultaneously increasing funding to the traditional structures of technology transfer like Max Planck and Fraunhofer institutes.

Similarly, firms have also adapted to a new paradigm learning with remarkable adeptness about equity markets and, accordingly, have grown in terms of market capitalisation significantly since the mid-1990s. They have bought large overseas companies as a means of entering markets and acquiring new know-how. And they have bought small high-tech ventures, particularly in the US and the UK, as a means of outsourcing the high risks attached to radical innovations.

It was the Deutsche Bank, the Dresdner Bank and the Hypo-Vereinsbank that first entered global markets at the beginning of the 1990s, through outward investment and through purchase. Other large German corporations followed their lead after a 'learning' time lag which included some notable false starts (Loewendahl 1999). Banks have ensured their own safety in riskier technology-based investments in small companies by using the technology transfer system (particularly Fraunhofer Institutes) to evaluate proposals. At the level of mentoring and support for small businesses, the nationally based INSTI network provides a resource to small businesses of lawyers, accountants, technology specialists, mentors and, ultimately, business angels and venture capital funds as a means of spurring SME growth through innovation.

It is, then, the disappointing record of the Schröder's first year which has given rise to the criticisms of Germany which have dominated commentary recently. There was so much hope that Schröder could rejuvenate the country within his first 100 days and the frustration with incoherence at the heart of policy has prompted the one-sidedly negative argument.

But where policy has been implemented to facilitate and to enable markets to operate effectively we would argue that it has been effective. Innovation policy is strong as are regional policies and small and medium-sized enterprise (SME) support policies. It is incredibly hard in a consensus-based society to change things overnight. We hope we have presented evidence that things are improving. Policy inconsistencies are becoming less marked and industrial policy is effective. The institutional structures provide deep-rooted and adaptable support to large and small companies alike. 'Light and Shade' is at the heart of the Performance Paradox of the German economy with which we started. The resolution to the paradox is in understanding the structural *flexibilities* in *Modell Deutschland* which give it a positive future.

Bibliography

Abraham, F. (1999): 'A Policy Perspective on European Unemployment' *Scottish Journal of Political Economy*, Vol. 46, No. 4, pp. 350–66.

Abramson, H., Norman, Encarnacao, J., Ried, P. and Schmoch, U. (eds) (1997): *Technology Transfer Systems in the United States and Germany: Lessons and Perspectives.* Washington, DC: National Academy Press.

Adelberger, K. (2000): 'Semi-Sovereign Leadership? The State's Role in German Biotechnology and Venture Capital Growth', *German Politics*, Vol. 9, No. 1, pp. 100–18.

Albert, M. (1993): *Capitalism Against Capitalism.* London: Whurr.

Amoore, L., Dodgson, R., Gills, B. K., Langley, P., Marshall, D. and Watson, I., (1997): 'Overturning Globalisation: Resisting the Teleological, Reclaiming the Political', *New Political Economy*, Vol. 2, No. 1, pp. 179–95.

Atkinson, A. B. (1993): *Welfare and Work Incentives: A North European Perspective.* Oxford: Clarendon.

Audretsch, D. B. (1999): 'Is the German Economic Model Still Viable?', *Wirtschaftspolitische Blätter*, Vol. 46, No. 3, pp. 276–85.

Augsdorfer, P. and Harding, R. (1995): 'Changing Competitive Forces in Europe: The Case of Continuous Improvement in a Sample of French, German and British Companies', *European Business Review*, Vol. 95, No. 4, pp. 3–9.

Augsdorfer, P. and Harding, R. (1996): 'Organisational Change and the Need for CI: Case Studies of Three European Countries', *European Business Review*, Vol. 96, No. 4, pp. 2–14.

Armingeon, Klaus (1991): 'Ende einer Erfolgsstory?: Gewerkschaften und Arbeitsbeziehungen im Einigungsprozeß', *Gegenwartskunde*, Vol. 40, No. 1, pp. 29–42.

Bamberg, U., Dzielak, W., Hindrichs, W. Martens, H. and Pter, G. (1984): *Praxis der Unternehmensmitbestimmung nach dem Mitbestimmungsgesetz, 1976 – eine Problemstudie.* Düsseldorf: Hans-Böckler Stiftung/Deutscher Gewerkschaftsbund.

Becher, G., Gering, T., Lang, O. and Schmoch, U. (1996): *Patentwesen an den Hochschulen: Eine Studie zum Stellenwert gewerblicher Schutzrechte im Tech-*

nologietransfer Hochschule-Wirtschaft. Bonn: BMBF.

Beck, U. (1992): *Risk Society*. London: Sage.

Becker, U. (1996): 'Beschäftigungswunderland Niederland?', *Aus Politik und Zeitgeschichte*, Vol. 48, No. 11, pp. 12–21.

Belitz, H. (1997): 'Research and Development in Multinational Companies from a German Perspective', *Economic Bulletin*, Vol. 34, No. 9, pp. 113–20.

Bell, D. (1961): *The End of Ideology*. New York: Collier.

Berger, S. and Dore, R. (eds) (1996): *National Diversity and Global Capitalism*. Ithaca: Cornell University Press.

Berthold, N. and Hank, R. (1999): *Bündnis für Arbeit: Korporatismus statt Wettbewerb*. Walter Eucken Institut, Beiträge zur Ordnungstheorie und Ordnungspolitik, No. 159. Tübingen: Mohr Siebeck.

Bertsch, F. (1997): *Wie gut ist der Wirtschaftstandort Deutschland? Die Globalisierung verschärft den Wettbewerb*. Internationes, Basis–Info (Wirtschaft). 3–97 No. 770Q8415. Bonn: IN-Press.

Bessant, J., Caffyn, S., Gilbert, J. and Harding, R. (1994): 'Rediscovering Continuous Improvement', *Technovation*, Vol. 14, No. 1, pp. 17–29.

Black, S. W. (1998): 'Globalization, Technological Change and the Welfare State', Economic Studies Program Conference Report No. 3, American Institute for Contemporary German Studies 1998. Washington: Johns Hopkins University.

Blank, R. (1994): *Social protection versus Economic Flexibility: Is There a Tradeoff?*. Chicago: University of Chicago Press.

Block, F. (1990): *Postindustrial Possibilities: A Critique of Economic Discourse*. Oxford: Oxford University Press.

BMBF (1999): 'Innoregio: innovative Impulse für die Region', Berlin, BMBF.

Boltho, A. (ed.) (1982): *The European Economy: Growth and Crisis*. Oxford, Oxford University Press.

Boyer, R. and Drache, D. (eds) (1996): *States Against Markets: The Limits of Globalisation*. London, Routledge.

Broyer, S. (1996): 'The Social Market Economy: Birth of an Economic Style', WZB discussion paper, FSI-96-318. Berlin: Wissenschaftszentrum.

Bulmer, S., Jeffery, C., and Paterson, W. E. (2000): *Germany's European Diplomacy: Shaping the Regional Milieu*. Manchester: Manchester University Press.

Bundesministerium für Arbeit und Sozialordnung (ed.) (1998): *Sozialpolitische Informationen*. Vol. 32, No. 18 pp. 1–2. Bonn: Bundesminsterium für Arbeit und Sozialordnung.

Cantwell, J. A. (1995): 'The Globalisation of Technology: What Remains of the Product Cycle Model?', *Cambridge Journal of Economics*, Vol. 19, No. 1, pp 155–74.

Cantwell, J. A. and Harding, R. (1998): 'The Internationalisation of German R&D', *National Institute Economic Review*, Vol. 1, No. 163, pp. 99–115.

Carlin, W. (1998): 'West Germany', in Foley, B. J. (ed.), *European Economies Since the Second World War*. London: Macmillan, pp. 25–47

Carlin, W. and Soskice, D. (1997): 'Shocks to the System: The German Political Economy under Stress' *National Institute Economic Review*, Vol. 1, No. 159 pp. 57–76.

Casper, S. (1998): 'National Institutional Frameworks and High-technology Innovation in Germany: The Case of Biotechnology'. Unpublished paper to Innovation Systems and Industrial Performance Workshop, Wissenschaftszentrum, Berlin, 23–4 October.

Casper, S., Lehrer, M. and Soskice, D. (1999): 'Can High Technology Industries Prosper in Germany? Institutional Frameworks and the Evolution of the German Software and Biotechnology Industries', *Industry and Innovation,* Vol. 6, No. 1, pp. 5–24.

Cerny, P. G. (1990): *The Changing Architecture of Politics: Structure, Agency and the Future of the State.* London: Sage.

Cerny, P. G. (1991): 'The Limits of Deregulation, Transnational Interpenetration and Policy Change', *European Journal of Political Research.* Vol. 19, No. 2, pp. 173–96.

Coates, D. (1999): 'Labour Power and international Competitiveness: A Critique of Ruling Orthodoxies', *Socialist Register*, pp. 108–41.

Coates, D. (2000): *Models of Capitalism. Growth and Stagnation in the Modern Era.* Cambridge: Polity Press.

Commission of the European Communities (CEC) (1993): *Growth, Competitiveness and Employment: The Challenges and Ways Forward into the 21st century.* White Paper, Brussels.

Crafts, N. F. R. (1999): 'The Great Boom: 1950–73' in Schulze, M.-S. (ed.), *Western Europe: Economic and Social Changes since 1945.* London and New York: Longman, pp. 42–62.

Crouch, C. (1997): 'Skills-based Full Employment: The Latest Philosopher's Stone', *British Journal of Industrial Relations*, Vol. 35, No. 3, pp. 367–91.

Crouch, C. and Streeck, W. (eds) (1997): *Political Economy of Modern Capitalism.* London: Sage.

Crowther, S., Hopkins, M., Martin, P., Millstone, E., Sharp, M. and van Zwangenberg, P. (1999): *Benchmarking Innovation in Modern Biotechnology.* Final Report to the European commission DGIII: Industry. Brighton, SPRU, University of Sussex.

Cusack, T. (1997): 'On the Road to Weimar? The Political Economy of Popular Satisfaction with Government and Regime Performance in Germany.' Wissenschaftszentrum Berlin, Discussion Paper No. FS-1 97–303.

Daly, A., Hitchins, D. M. and Wagner, K. (1985): 'Productivity, Machinery and Skills in a Sample of British and German Manufacturing Plants: Results of a Pilot Enquiry', *National Institute Economic Review*, No. III, pp. 48–61.

Davidson, I. (1997): *Jobs and the Rhineland Model.* London: Federal Trust for Education and Research.

Davis, P. and Reich, S. (1999): 'Norms, Ideology, and Institutions: (En)Gendered

Retrenchment of *Modell Deutschland*?', in Brady, J. S., Crawford, B. and Williarty, S. E. (eds), *The Post-war Transformation of Germany: Democracy, Prosperity and Nationhood*. Ann Arbor: University of Michigan Press, pp. 225–67.

Deutsche Bundesbank (1999): *Economic Conditions in Germany*, Monthly Report, August, pp. 28–38. Frankfurt: Deutsche Bundesbank.

Deutsches Institut fuer Wirtschaftsforschung (DIW) (1999): 'The German Economy in the Autumn of 1999', *Economic Bulletin*, Vol. 37, No. 11. Heidelberg, Springer Verlag. Internet www.diw.de/diwwbe/

Deutsches Institut fuer Wirtschaftsforschung (DIW) (2000): German Economic Trends, Economic Bulletin, Vol. 37, No. 1/2000, Internet www.diw.de/diwwbe/

Der Spiegel (44/1999): Hamburg: Spiegel Verlag, pp. 22–30.

Der Spiegel (7/2000): Hamburg: Spiegel Verlag, pp. 86–9.

Dorscht, A. (1988): 'Concerted Action: Labour's Corporatist Strategy in the Federal Republic of Germany, 1967–1977', unpublished Ph.D. thesis, Ottawa, Carleton University.

Drucker, P. (1986): 'The Changed World Economy' *Foreign Affairs*, Vol. 64, No. 4, pp. 768–91.

Dunning, J. H. (1995): 'Re-appraising the Eclectic Paradigm in the Age of Alliance Capitalism', EMOT Workshop, University of Reading, 14–16 May.

Duysters, G. and Hagedoorn, J. (1996): 'Internationalisation of Corporate Technology through Strategic Partnering: An Empirical Investigation' *Research Policy*, Vol. 25, No. 1, pp. 1–25.

Dyson, K. (1999): 'German Economic Policy after Fifty Years' in Merkl, P. H. (ed.), *The Federal Republic of Germany at Fifty. The End of a Century of Turmoil.* Hampshire and London: Macmillan, pp. 219–30.

Dyson, K. (2000): 'The Euro and its Impact on European Member States' Unpublished Working Paper to the Sussex European Institute, 22 February.

Dyson, K. and Featherstone, K. (1999): *The Road to Maastricht: Negotiating Economic and Monetary Union*. Oxford: Oxford University Press.

Economist, The (1988): 'Wunderkind at 40', 7 May1998. London: *The Economist.*

Economist, The (1998): Leader columns, week beginning, 7 Nov. 1998. London: *The Economist.*

Economist, The (2000): 'Free to Bloom', pp. 17–19. London: *The Economist.*

Economist Intelligence Unit (2000): *Germany: Country Report*, first quarter 2000, London.

Eichengreen, B. and Iversen, T. (1999): 'Institutions and Economic Performance: Evidence from the Labour Market', in *Oxford Review of Economic Policy*, Vol. 15, No. 4, pp. 121–38.

Esping-Andersen, G. (1994): 'Welfare States and the Economy', in Smelser, N. and Swedberg, R. (eds), *The Handbook of Economic Sociology*. Princeton, NJ: Princeton University Press.

Esser, J. and Schröder, W. (1999): 'Neues Leben fur den Rheinischen Kapitalismus: Vom Bündnis für Arbeit zum Dritten Weg', *Blätter fur deutsche und internationale Politik*, No. 1, pp. 51–61.

Eucken, W. (1952/1982): 'A Policy for Establishing a System of Free Enterprise' in Erhard-Stiftung, L. (ed.): *Standard Texts on the Social Market Economy*, Stuttgart, New York: Gustav Fischer, pp. 115–31.

European Industrial Relations Review (EIRR), various issues.

Fichter, M. (1997): 'Trade Union Members: A Vanishing Species in Post-unification Germany?', *German Studies Review*, Vol. 20, No. 1, pp. 88–104.

Fichter, M. and Reister, H. (1996): 'Die Gewerkschaften', in Niedermayer, O. (ed.), *Intermediäre Strukturen in Ostdeutschland*, Opladen: Leske und Budrich, pp. 1–27.

Financial Times (2000): 17.02.00. London, Pitman Group.

Fitzroy, F. R., Acs, Z. J. and Gerlowski, D. A. (1998): *Management and Economics of Organisation*, Harlow: Pearson Education.

Fraunhofer Gesellschaft (1997): *Die Fraunhofer Gesellschaft im Profil: Auftrag, Leistung, Perspektiven*. Munich: Fraunhofer Gesellschaft.

Freeman, C. (1995): 'The "National System of Innovation" in Historical Perspective', *Cambridge Journal of Economics*, Vol. 19 (February), pp. 4–24.

Freeman, R. B. (1994): *Working Under Different Rules*. London: Russell Sage Foundation.

French, S. (1999): 'A "Third Way" through Social Pacts? Trade Union Weakness and the Limits of German Corporatism', in Funk, L. (ed.), *The Economics and the Politics of the Third Way: Essays in Honour of Eric Owen Smith*. Hamburg: Lit-Verlag, pp. 99–116

Funk, L. (1999): 'Labour Market Dynamics in Western Europe and the USA', in Filc, W. and Koehler, C. (eds), *Macreconomic Causes of Unemployment: Diagnosis and Policy Recommendations*. Berlin: Duncker & Humblot, pp. 189–225.

Giddens, A. (1998): *The Third Way*. Cambridge: Polity Press.

Giersch, H., Paqué, K. -H. and Schmieding, H. (1992): *The Fading Miracle: Four Decades of Market Economy in Germany*. Cambridge: Cambridge University Press

Goethe, J. W. von (1949): *Faust*. Part I. Reprinted 1978, translation by Philip Wagner. London: Penguin,

Goodhart, D. (1994): *The Reshaping of the German Social Market*. London: Institute for Public Policy Research.

Graham, A. (1997): 'The UK 1979–95: Myths and Realities of Conservative Capitalism', in Crouch, C. and Streeck, W. (eds), *Political Economy of Modern Capitalism*, London: Sage, pp. 117–32.

Grant, W., Paterson, W. and Whitson, C. (1988): *Government and the Chemical Industry: A comparative Study of Britain and West Germany*. Oxford: Clarendon.

Hancké, B. (1997): 'Reconfiguring the German Production System: Crisis and Adjustment in the Automobile Industry'. Paper presented to workshop on '*Modell Deutschland* in the 1990s', Wissenschaftszentrum Berlin, 27–28 June, 1997.

Hank, R. (1996): 'Der Zauberer: Bündnis für Arbeit statt Programmdebatte', *Gewerkschaftliche Monatshefte*, Vol. 47, No. 1, pp. 32–40.

Harding, R. (1995): *Technology and Human Resource Strategies in their National Context: A Study of Strategic Contrasts.* Aldershot: Avebury.

Harding, R. (1996): 'Implementing Strategic Change: A Study of British and German Workers', *Technovation*, Vol .16, No. 2, pp. 101–13.

Harding, R. (1999a): 'Standort Deutschland: An End to the Economic Miracle?', *German Politics*, Vol. 8, No. 1, pp. 66–88.

Harding, R. (1999b): *Venture Capital and Regional Development.* London: IPPR.

Hasse, R. H. (1999): 'Beschäftigungspolitik. Von überfrachteter Normativität zu mehr Pragmatismus mit Mängeln?', *Zeitschrift zur politischen Bildung* Eichholz Brief, Vol. 36, No. 3, pp. 57–65.

Hassel, A. (1998): 'Soziale Pakte in Europa', *Gewerkschaftliche Monatshefte*, Vol. 10, pp. 626–38.

Hassel, A. (1999): 'The Erosion of the German System of Industrial Relations', *British Journal of Industrial Relations*, Vol. 37, No. 3, pp. 483–505.

Hassel, A. and Schulten, T. (1998): 'Globalization and the Future of Central Collective Bargaining: The Example of the German Metal Industry', *Economy and Society*, Vol. 27, No. 4, pp. 486–52.

Hefeker, C. (1998): 'Globalization and the "German Model": Can It Survive?', in Black, S. (ed.) *Globalization, Technological Change, and Labour Markets.* Dordrecht: Kluwer Academic Publishers, pp. 141–77

Heise, A. (1997): 'The British and German Models of Labour Market Regulation Compared'. Unpublished paper presented to ICLS Conference on 'European Systems of Labour Market Regulation', UMIST, 31 January.

Herrigel, G. (1994): 'A Surprise Crisis in German Decentralised Production: Unexpected Rigidity and the Challenge of an Alternative Form of Flexible Organisation in the 1990s', Draft paper, University of Chicago, 14 September.

Hilferding, R. (1981): *Finance Capital: A Study of the Latest Phase of Capitalist Development.* London: Routledge and Kegan Paul.

Hirst, P. and Thompson, G. (1996): *Globalisation in Question.* Cambridge: Polity Press.

Hohn, H. W. (1998): *Steuerungsprobleme und kognitive Strukturen der Forschung: Kernphysik und Informatik im Vergleich.* Köln: Max Planck Institut für Gesellschaftsforschung.

Hohn, H. W. (1999): 'Projektskizze zur Funktionsweise und institutioneller Wandel nationaler Innovationssysteme. Das Fallbeispiel der Gemeinschaftsforschung im internationalen Vergleich'. Unpublished mimeograph. Köln: Max Planck Institut für fuer Gesellschaftsforschung.

Hohn, H. W. and Schimank, U. (1990): *Konflikte und Gleichgewichte im Forschungssystem: Akteurskonstellationen und Entwicklungspfade in der staatlich finanzierten ausseruniversitaeren Forschung.* Frankfurt: Campus Verlag.

Hollingsworth, J. R. and Boyer, R. (eds) (1997): *Contemporary Capitalism: The*

Embeddedness of Institutions. Cambridge: Cambridge University Press.

Hutton, W. (1995): *The State We're In*. Aldershot: Edward Elgar.

IMF–International Monetary Fund (1999a): 'Germany: Staff Report for the 1999 Article IV Consultation', *IMF Staff Country Report*, No. 99/129, Washington.

IMF–International Monetary Fund (1999b): *World Economic Outlook*, May, Washington.

IMF–International Monetary Fund (1999c): *World Economic Outlook*, October, Washington.

Institut der Deutschen Wirtschaft (1997): *Arbeitszeitflexibilisierung: Notwendigkeiten, Hemmnisse, Möglichkeiten*, Köln: Institut der Deutschen Wirtschaft.

Jeffery, C. (1999): 'Party Politics and Territorial Representation in the Federal Republic of Germany', *West European Politics*, Vol. 22, No. 2, pp. 130–66.

Jessop, B. (1994): 'Post-Fordism and the State', in Amin, A. (ed.) *Post-Fordism: A Reader*, Oxford: Blackwell, pp. 251–79.

Jones, R. J. Barry. (1995): *Globalisation and Interdependence in the International Political Economy*. London: Pinter.

Kerr, C., Dunlop, J. T, Harbison, F. and Myers. C. (1962): *Industrialism and Industrial Man*, Cambridge, MA: Harvard University Press.

Kittner, M. (1992): 'Zur Situation in AEG', *Die Mitbestimmung* 6/92. Düsseldorf: Hans-Böckler Stiftung.

Kluth, M. and Andersen, J. (1997): 'Pooling the Technology Base', in Howells, J. and Michie, J. (eds), *Technology, Innovation and Competitiveness*. Aldershot: Edward Elgar, pp. 65–88.

Knappe, E. (1998): 'Arbeitsmarktordnung und Arbeitsmarktpolitik', *Jahrbücher für. Nationalökonomie und Statistik*, Vol. 216, No. 4/5, pp. 498–523.

Knappe, E., Optendrenk, S., and Zimmermann, T. (1999): 'Does a Third Way exist for Germany's Statutory Health Insurance System?', in Funk, L. (ed.), *The Economics and the Politics of the Third Way. Essays in Honour of Eric Owen Smith*. Hamburg: Lit-Verlag, pp. 152–70.

Krull, W. and Meyer-Kramer, F. (1999): *Science and Technology in Germany*. London: John Harper Publishing.

Lane, C . (1989): *Management and Labour in Europe: The Industrial Enterprise in Germany, Britain and France.*' Aldershot: Edward Elgar.

Lazonick, W. (1991): *Business Organisation and the Myth of the Market Economy*. Cambridge: Cambridge University Press.

Lenin, V. I. (1982): *Imperialism: the Highest Stage of Capitalism*. Moscow: Progress Publishers.

Lissenburgh, S. and Harding, R. (2000): *Knowledge Links: Innovation in University/Business Partnerships*, London: IPPR.

Löckener, R. and Westphal, T. (1996): 'Bündnis fur Arbeit: Aufstieg und Fall?', *Zeitschrift fur Sozialistische Politik und Wirtschaft*, No. 89, pp. 12–15.

Lowendahl, H. (1999): 'Siemens' "Anglo-Saxon" Strategy: Is Globalising Business

Enough?', *German Politics*, Vol. 8, No. 1., pp. 89–105.
Mahnkopf, B. (1991): 'Vorwärts in die Vergangenheit?: Pessimistische Spekulationen über die Zukunft der Gewerkschaften in der neuen Bundesrepublik'. In Westphal, A. *et al.* (eds), *Wirtschaftspolitische Konsequenzen der deutschen Vereinigung*. Frankfurt-am-Main: Campus, pp. 269–94.
Mahnkopf, B. (1999): 'Between the Devil and the Deep Blue Sea: The German Model Under the Pressure of Globalisation', *Socialist Register*, pp. 142–77.
Markovits, A. S. (1986): *The Politics of the West German Trade Unions: Strategies of Class and Interest Representation in Growth and Crisis*. London: Macmillan.
Marsh, D. (1999): Germany's economy: Is the heart of Europe about to fail, *GBF-Review*, December, Internet www.gbf.com
Mason, G. and Wagner, K. (1994): 'Innovation and the Skills Mix: Chemicals and Engineering in Britain and Germany', *National Institute Economic Review*, No. 148, pp. 61–72.
Mason, G. and Wagner, K. (1999): 'Knowledge Transfer and Innovation in Germany and Britain: "Intermediate Institution" Models of Knowledge Transfer under Strain?', *Industry and Innovation*, Vol. 6, No. 1, pp 85–109.
Mason, G., von Ark, B. amd Wagner, K. (1994): 'Productivity, Product Quality and Workforce Skills: Food Processing in Four European Countries', *National Institute Economic Review*, No. 148, pp. 48–61.
Maurice, M., Sellier, F. and Silvestre, J. J. (1986): '*The Social Foundations of Industrial Power: A Comparison of France and Germany*.' Cambridge, MA: MIT Press.
Mayer, C. J. and Whittington, R. (1999): 'Strategy, Structure and 'Systemness': National Institutions and Corporate Change in France, Germany and the UK, 1950–1993', *Organisation Studies*, Vol. 20, No. 6, pp. 933–59.
Milward, A. S. and Saul, S. B. (1979): *The Economic Development of Continental Europe, 1780–1870*.' Second edition, London: Allen and Unwin.
Müller, H. and Wilke, M. (1999): *Rückkehr in die politische Arena: Die deutschen Gewerkschaften und das Bündnis für Arbeit*. Sankt Augustin: Konrad–Adenauer–Stiftung, Interne Studien 177.
OECD (1996): *Employment Outlook*, 12 July, Paris: OECD.
OECD (1999): *Economic Outlook*, 65, June, Paris: OECD.
OECD (1999a): Economic Survey Germany 1999, Paris.
OECD (1999b): Employment Outlook, June, Paris.
Ohmae, K. (1996): *The End of the Nation State: The Rise of Regional Economies*. London: HarperCollins.
Overbeek, H. (1990): *Global Capitalism and National Decline: The Thatcher Decade in Perspective*. London: Unwin Hyman.
Owen Smith, E. and Funk, L. (1994): 'Trade', in Owen Smith E. (ed.), *The German Economy*. London: Routledge, pp. 499–522.
Palan, R. and Abbott, J. (1996): *State Strategies in the Global Political Economy*. London: Pinter.
Paqué, K.-H. (1999): 'Structural Unemployment and Real Wage Rigidity in Ger-

many', *Kieler Studien*, 301. Tübingen: Mohn Siebeck.

Pfirrman, O. and Feldman, M. (1998): 'The Diffusion of Knowledge in Biotechnology: A Comparative Investigation of Berlin-Brandenburg and Baltimore-Washington', Freie Universität, Berlin, Working Paper, 1/98.

Pohl, R. (2000): 'East German Transformation: Success versus Failure?' Unpublished paper to the Institute for German Studies, 14 February.

Porter, H. (1999): 'Drink, Dance, It's All Over', *The Guardian*, 3 November.

Prais, S. (1981): *Productivity and Industrial Structure: A Statistical Study of Manufacturing in Britain, Germany and the US.* Cambridge: Cambridge University Press.

Prais, S. (1991): *The Evolution of Giant Firms in Britain, Germany and America.* Cambridge: Cambridge University Press.

Price Pritchett (1994): *New Work Habits for a Radically Changing World.* Tyne and Wear: Pritchett and Associates.

Randelsome, C. (1994): *The Business Culture in Germany: Portrait of a Powerhouse.* London: Butterworth-Heinemann.

Reich, R. (1991): *The Work of Nations: Preparing Ourselves for Twenty-first Century Capitalism.* New York: Alfred Knopf.

Reich, R. (1995): 'Who Is Us?', in Lazonick, W. and Mass, W. (eds), *Organisational Capability and competitive Advantage: Debates, dynamics and policy.* Aldershot: Edward Elgar, pp. 587–98.

Rhodes, M. (1997): 'Globalisation, Labour Markets and Welfare States: A Future of Competitive Corporatism?' in Rhodes, M. and Meny, Y. (eds), *The Future of European Welfare: A New Social Contract?* London: Macmillan.

Rubery, J. (1993): 'The UK Production Regime in Comparative Perspective'. Unpublished conference paper at conference on 'Production Regimes in an Integrating Europe', UMIST, Manchester.

Ruigrok, W. and Van Tulder, R. (1995): *The Logic of International Restructuring: The Management of Dependencies in Rival Industrial Complexes.* London: Routledge.

Sally, R. (1994): 'Multinational Enterprises, Political Economy and Institutional Theory: Domestic Embeddedness in the Context of Internationalization'. *Review of International Political Economy*, Vol. 1, No. 1, pp. 163–92.

Scharpf, F. W. (1998): 'The German Disease', *Prospect*, Internet: www.prospect-magazine.co.uk/highlights/german_disease/index.html

Schmidt, M. G. (1987): West Germany: The Policy of the Middle Way, *Journal of Public Policy*, Vol. 7, pp. 135–77.

Schmieding, H. (1999): 'Schröder Must Get Radical', *Wall Street Journal Europe*, 17.3.99, p. 10.

Schmoch, U. (1998): 'Interaction of Universities and Industrial Enterprises in Germany and the United States: A Comparison'. Unpublished Paper to 'Innovation Systems and Industrial Performance' workshop, Wissenschaftszentrum, Berlin, 23–4 October.

Schröder, G. (1999): 'Das Modell Deutschland ist nicht überholt', *Frankfurter Allgemeine Zeitung*, 25.9.99, pp. 7–8.
Schröder, W. and Esser, J. (1999): '*Modell Deutschland*: Von der Konzertierten Aktion zum Bündnis für Arbeit', *Aus Politik und Zeitgeschichte*, Vol. 49, No. 37, pp. 3–12.
Schröder, W. und Burkhard, R. (1996): *Austritte aus Arbeitgeberverbänden* 'Motive – Ursachen – Ausmass', *WSI Mitteilungen*, Vol. 49, No. 5, pp. 316–29.
Scott, J. (1997): *Corporate Business and Capitalist Classes.* Oxford: Oxford University Press.
Seccombe, W. (1999): 'Contradictions of Shareholder Capitalism: Downsizing Jobs, Enlisting Savings, Destabilizing Families', *Socialist Register*, pp. 76–107.
Seidel, B./Vesper, D. (1999): 'Fiscal Federalism: An International Comparison', *DIW Discussion Paper*, No. 183, April, Berlin.
Shonfeld, A. (1969): *Modern Capitalism: The Changing Balance of Public and Private Power* Oxford: Oxford University Press.
Siebert, H. (1999a): 'How Competitive is Europe's Labour?', *Kiel Working Paper*, No. 927, Kiel Institute of World Economics, May.
Siebert, H. (1999b): *The World Economy*, London and New York: Routledge.
Silvia, S. (1993): 'Holding the Shop Together: Old and New Challenges to the German System of Industrial Relations in the mid-1990s', *Berliner Arbeitshefte und Berichte zur sozialwissenschaftlichen Forschung*, Discussion Paper No. 83. Berlin. Freie Universität.
Silvia, S. (1999): 'Every Which Way but Loose: German Industrial Relations since 1980', in Martin, A. and Ross, G. (eds), *The Brave New World of European Labour: European Trade Unions at the Millennium.* Oxford. Berghahn, pp. 74–124.
Somers, F. (1998): *European Union Economies. A Comparative Study.* Harlow: Addison Wesley.
Sorge, A. (1999): 'Mitbestimmung, Arbeitsorganisation und Technikanwendung', in Streeck, W. and Kluge, N. (eds), *Mitbestimmung in Deutschland: Tradition und Effizienz.* Frankfurt: Campus Verlag, pp. 17–134.
Soskice, D. (1994): 'Innovation strategies of Companies: A Comparative Institutional Approach of Some Cross-Country Differences'. In Zapf, W. and Dierkes, M. (eds), *Institutionenvergleich und Institutionendynamik.* WZB Jahrbuch, Berlin, WZB, pp. 271–89.
Soskice, D. (1996): 'German Technology Policy, Innovation and National Institutional Frameworks', WZB Discussion Paper, FS 1-96-319, Berlin: Wissenschaftszentrum.
Stopford, J. and Strange, S. (1991): *Rival States, Rival Firms: Competition for World Market Shares.* New York: Cambridge University Press.
Strange, S. (1996): *The Retreat of the State: The Diffusion of Power in the World Economy.* Cambridge: Cambridge University Press.
Streeck, W. (1992): *Social Institutions and Economic Performance: Studies of Indus-*

trial Relations in Advanced Capitalist Economies. London: Sage.

Streeck, W. (1997): 'German Capitalism: Does it Exist? Can it Survive?', *New Political Economy,* Vol. 2, No. 2, pp. 237–56.

Streeck, W. (1998a): 'Bündnis fur Arbeit: Bedingungen und Ziele', *Gewerkschaftliche Monatshefte,* Vol. 49, No. 8, pp. 533–40.

Streeck, W. (1998b): 'The Internationalization of Industrial Relations in Europe: Prospects and Problems', *Politics and Society,* Vol. 26, No. 4, pp. 429–59.

Streeck, W. (1999): 'Drohgesten sind von gestern', *Einblick,* No. 3, p. 3.

Streeck, W. and Kluge, N. (eds) (1999): *Mitbestimmung in Deutschland: Tradition und Effizienz.* Frankfurt: Campus Verlag.

SVR–Council of Economic Experts (1998): 'Facing Far-reaching Decisions'. Internet www.Sachverstaendigenrat-Wirtschaft.de/jg98/engl98.htm

SVR–Council of Economic Experts (1999): 'Wirtschaftspolitik unter Reformdruck'. Internet www.Sachverstaendigenrat-Wirtschaft.de

Technologie Nachrichten (1998): March issue, Hamburg.

Timmins, G. (2000): *German Unification and Organised Labour: Social Partnership under Pressure.* Manchester: Manchester University Press.

Turner, L. (1998): *Fighting for Partnership: Labour and Politics in Unified Germany.* Cornell: Cornell University Press.

Upchurch, M. (1998): 'The Rise and Fall of *Modell Deutschland*', Mimeo.

Van der Pijl, K., (1984): *The Making of an Atlantic Ruling Class.* London: Verso.

Vitols, S. (1997): 'German Industrial Policy: An Overview', *Industry and Innovation,* Vol. 4, No. 1, pp. 15–36.

Vogel, S. V. (1996): *Freer markets, More Rules: Regulatory Reform in Advanced Industrialised Countries.* Ithaca: Cornell University Press.

Watrin, C. (1999): 'Germany's Social Market Economy'. In Kilmarnock, A. (ed.), *The Social Market and the State, Social Market Foundation.* London: Profile Books, pp. 89–104

Watson, M. and Hay, C. (1998): 'In the Dedicated Pursuit of Dedicated Capital: Restoring an Indigenous Investment Ethic to British Capitalism', *New Political Economy,* Vol. 3, No. 3, pp. 407–26.

Webster, F. (1995): *Theories of the information Society.* London: Routledge.

Weiss, L. (1998): *The Myth of the Powerless State: Governing the Economy in a Global Era.* Cambridge: Polity Press.

Weßels, B. (1999): 'Die deutsche Variante des Korporatismus'. In Kaase, M. and Schmid, G. (eds), *Eine lernende Demokratie: 50 Jahre Bundesrepublik Deutschland.* WZB-Jahrbuch, Berlin: Edition Sigma, pp. 87–113.

Wever, K. (1995): *Negotiating Competitiveness: Employment Relations and Organizational Innovation in Germany and the United States.* Boston, MA: Harvard Business School Press.

Wijnbergen, C. van (1999): 'The Politics of Reforms: Battling Unemployment in Germany and the Netherlands'. Paper presented at American Political Science Association Annual Conference, Atlanta, Georgia.

Wirtschaftswoche (10 Feb. 2000): 'Erst am Anfang – Deutschland steht vor weiteren feindlichen übernahmen – viele Grosskonzerne haben den Anschluss an die Weltspitze verpasst', No. 7, pp. 50–6.

Wolf, M. (1999): Making Europe work, *Financial Times*, 27 July 1999, p. 16. London: *Financial Times.*

Womak, J. P., Jones, D. and Roos, D. (1990): *The Machine that Changed the World.* New York: MIT Press.

World Bank, (1995): 'Workers in an Integrating World'. *World Development Report.* Oxford: Oxford University Press.

Zumwinkle, M. (1995): 'Standort Deutschland: Can a Changing Germany Compete in the Changing World Market?', in Shingleton, A. *et al.*. (eds), *Dimensions of German Unification: Economic, Social and Legal Analyses.* Oxford: Westview, pp. 71–87.

Zwickel, K. (1996): 'Bündnis für Arbeit: Prinzipien – Probleme – Perspektiven', in Fricke, W. (ed.), *Jahrbuch Arbeit und Technik 1996.* Bonn: Dietz.

Zysman, J. (1996): 'The Myth of Global Economy: Enduring National Foundations and Emerging Regional Realities', *New Political Economy*, Vol. 1, No. 2, pp. 157–84.

Index